Interbehaviorism

A Comprehensive Guide To The Foundations Of Kantor's Theory And Its Applications For Modern Behavior Analysis

Linda J. Hayes, PhD
Mitch J. Fryling, PhD

16pt

Read How You Want
LARGE PRINT BOOKS, BRAILLE & DAISY

Copyright Page from the Original Book

Publisher's Note

This publication is designed to provide accurate and authoritative information in regard to the subject matter covered. It is sold with the understanding that the publisher is not engaged in rendering psychological, financial, legal, or other professional services. If expert assistance or counseling is needed, the services of a competent professional should be sought.

NEW HARBINGER PUBLICATIONS is a registered trademark of New Harbinger Publications, Inc.

New Harbinger Publications is an employee-owned company.

Context Press
An imprint of New Harbinger Publications, Inc.
5674 Shattuck Avenue
Oakland, CA 94609
www.newharbinger.com

Cover design by Amy Shoup; Acquired by Ryan Buresh;
Edited by Karen Levy; Indexed by James Minkin

Library of Congress Cataloging-in-Publication Data on file

TABLE OF CONTENTS

TABLE OF CONTENTS

"This book clarifies Kantor's comprehensive philosophy of a science of behavior/environment relations. Pragmatically, understanding the interrelations of the operant and history of instruction of development, setting events, and phylogeny is simply fundamental to successful applied work, not unlike Israel Goldiamond's clinical systems analyses. Current exciting work in the basic and applied/basic science is doing that. This book is timely, and a necessary text for courses on 'concepts and principles of behavior.'"

—**R. Douglas Greer, PhD, CABAS SBA, SRS,** professor of psychology and education at Columbia University Teachers College and Graduate School of Arts and Sciences

"*Interbehaviorism* by Linda Hayes and Mitch Fryling is not only an introductory text to the logic and categories of interbehaviorism as formulated by J.R. Kantor almost a century ago. It is also a comprehensive conceptual analysis of the nature of psychological theory, and its relationship with research, application, and interpretation. The book focuses mainly on comparing interbehavioral concepts with those of traditional dualistic theories and with operant psychology analyses. Elegant examples are provided on varied topics related to human behavior, such as language, memory, feelings, and development, among others. This is a very needed text in the field in order to provide conceptual awareness not only to newcomers and students, but also to experienced researchers and teachers."

> **—Emilio Ribes-Iñesta, PhD,** researcher at the University of Veracruz at Xalapa (Mexico), devoted to theoretical and experimental analysis of psychological behavior from the standpoint of field theory

"Hayes and Fryling offer a valuable contribution to the understanding of J.R. Kantor's philosophy and its relevance to the investigation, application, and interpretation of behavioral phenomena. *Interbehaviorism* brings a comprehensive perspective of the complexity involved in systems where behavior is embedded. It adds to Skinner's inductive analysis of behavior as a function of the environment. This book should be required reading for students of behavior analysis."

> **—Maria E. Malott, PhD,** CEO of the Association for Behavior Analysis International, who publishes on analyses of complex cultural phenomena from a behavioral science perspective

"Although I didn't realize it, I've been waiting for this book for most of my academic career.

And having read it, I now find that I am, philosophically, more of a Kantorian than a Skinnerian. But this work is also critically important for those outside of behaviorism, and indeed academic psychology writ large. Anyone with an interest in science and/or philosophy should study this wonderfully crafted, scholarly, and erudite text."

—**Dermot Barnes-Holmes,** professor of psychology at Ulster University, and fellow of the Association for Behavior Analysis International and the Association for Contextual Behavioral Science

"Hayes and Fryling provide an extended overview of interbehavioral psychology and its foundational contribution to the science of behavior. Their discussion of interdisciplinary science offers a timely context for our examination of the current and future practices in behavior science. Moreover, their outstanding review of the interbehavioral concepts and implicit responding highlight implications of this approach for research and practice. Important read for academicians, researchers, and practitioners in behavior science."

—**Ramona A. Houmanfar, PhD,** professor of psychology and director of the behavior analysis program at the University of Nevada, Reno; author of over eighty articles; and coeditor of three books

"This book is the clearest primer of the interbehavioral position ever written. While interbehaviorism has been a recognizable strand within behavioral psychology for the last century, many find J.R. Kantor hard to read and to understand. In the modern day, field theoretical concepts and the analytic tools needed to measure and study them are gaining traction. Written by two of the foremost living interbehavioral scholars, for students and others unfamiliar with Kantor's effort at system building, there is no better place to begin."

—Steven C. Hayes, PhD, Nevada Foundation Professor of psychology at the University of Nevada, Reno

We dedicate this book to all those who have expressed an interest in learning more about interbehaviorism and interbehavioral psychology. We wrote this book for you.

Introduction

Jacob Robert Kantor's (1888–1984) doctoral degree was awarded by the University of Chicago in 1917, his dissertation entitled *The Functional Nature of the Philosophical Categories*. Upon receiving his degree, he served as an instructor at the University of Chicago until 1920, and then took a position at the University of Indiana. During his time at the University of Indiana, he founded *The Psychological Record,* in which he published more than fifty comments and queries under the nom de plume of "Observer." He overlapped briefly with B.F. Skinner during this period. Upon retiring from the University of Indiana in 1959, he returned to the University of Chicago as an emeritus member of the faculty, where, over the next forty-five years, he added numerous papers on interbehaviorism and interbehavioral psychology to his resume (a complete bibliography of Kantor's works is available at http://www.newharbinger.com/46837). In other words, Kantor's contributions to a natural science of psychology and to the philosophy of science were voluminous even after his retirement. They were also wide in scope, featuring works on physiological psychology (e.g., 1947), logic (1945–1950), history of science (e.g., 1963–1969), linguistics (e.g., 1977), philosophy (e.g., 1981), cultural psychology (e.g., 1982), and tragedy (1983), among many other topics.

Kantor's goals for philosophy, science, and psychology were obviously pursued in all of his works on these topics. In the case of philosophy, his aim was to build a system in which presuppositions of absolutism, universalism, and finalism, common to all traditional philosophical systems, were eliminated (e.g., Kantor, 1981). For science, and the science of psychology in particular, his goal was to ensure the internal consistency of scientific constructions and their coherence with those of other sciences (Kantor, 1953), and to promote comprehensive coverage of their subject matters (Kantor, 1970), by fostering the practice of system building and eliminating the presupposition of dualism.

Despite the wealth of his contributions to the development of a naturalistic philosophy and science of behavior, Kantor's work is not well known relative to others of the behavioral tradition, including B.F. Skinner—and possibly because of him. Skinner was an experimentalist, initially working with pigeons. From these experiments, principles of behavior (e.g., reinforcement, extinction, stimulus control) were abstracted and anointed with causal properties. These, in turn, became the wherewithal for the development of an applied science. Skinner's radical behaviorism is not a fully developed philosophy though, and Skinner was not a philosopher. By contrast, Kantor considered himself to be a philosopher (Hass, 1984), and while he was exceptionally well informed as to the nature of investigation (Kantor, 1953, 1958), he did not personally conduct experiments or applications based on their findings.

We suspect that this circumstance contributed substantially to the fact that Kantor's work was overlooked or ignored for so many decades of the last century. Experimentalists tend to overvalue investigation at the expense of theory and practice. They have also been convinced that theory and philosophy are unnecessary—or worse, harmful—features of scientific enterprises. The latter is a legitimate claim when theories and philosophies are imbued with propositions derived from nonnatural sources. But Kantor's philosophy is not of this sort, and it is necessary for the continued development of a natural science of behavior.

In more recent times, the scientific community has come to value the work of philosophers in sustaining the adequacy and ensuring the comprehensiveness of its scientific systems. With this realization has come a greater interest in Kantor's work. Some behaviorists have even suggested that there might be a way for Kantor's and Skinner's works to be combined into a single system. The idea here is that perhaps a new science of behavior could be developed in which interbehaviorism would constitute its philosophical foundation, and its investigative and applied work would be derived from Skinner's behavior analysis. Some arrangement of investigative practices and its products, derived from the work of Skinner, might be incorporated into the investigative and applied subsystems of interbehavioral psychology, as discussed in chapters 4 and 5. However, they would not be able to be interpreted in the manner characteristic of radical behaviorism because they would be founded on different philosophical assumptions. This is to say, while Kantor's interbehaviorism and Skinner's radical behaviorism are both naturalistic in kind, they are not alike at a fundamental level. Specifically, Kantor's integrated field construction, which admits of no causes of any sort (i.e., forceful or selective) operating from any location (i.e., internal or external) or in any time frame (i.e., history or future), is incompatible with Skinner's causal contingency formulation.

It's not just the issue of causality that distinguishes interbehaviorism from radical behaviorism though; the elements comprising the subject matter of each are conceptualized differently as well. For example, **stimulus objects** are distinguished from their functions in Kantor's system, and it is always their functions that are entailed in behavior segments. From a radical behavioral perspective, it is a stimulus object that fulfills this role. Likewise, the response factor is understood differently across the two perspectives. Both are focused on the functions of responses but, for radical behaviorists, the functions of responses are their presumed causes, while for interbehaviorists, response functions are analytical aspects of their interrelations with stimulus functions. Further, while both radical behaviorists and interbehaviorists purport to consider the whole organism to be the actor in a psychological event, this commitment is not always upheld by radical behaviorists.

Even the setting or context in which responding with respect to stimulating takes place is treated differently across the two positions. In radical behavioral thinking, the setting is essentially the cause of a cause, otherwise known as a conditional discrimination. In interbehavioral thinking, the setting is not the cause of other factors comprising the event field. Rather, it is a participating factor in that field. And, finally, interbehaviorists conceptualize setting factors as sources by way of which the organism's history is brought to bear in the present. By contrast, radical behaviorists assume that an organism's history is carried into the present by way of changes to its biological organs and tissues. In sum, Kantor's interbehaviorism and Skinner's radical behaviorism, upon which their interpretations of the very subject matter of behavior science are formulated, are not the same. To substantiate these arguments, and to accomplish our aim of clarifying Kantor's position on such matters, we have sometimes found it useful to compare his views with those of Skinner.

For the most part, though, we have sought to share our knowledge of Kantor's system with the aim of making it more accessible to unfamiliar readers. This book, as such, is a primer. Still, we have tried to do justice to Kantor's work, to stay as close to his original writings as possible, and to include our own works as extensions of his thinking. Finally, as mentioned above, Kantor was an extremely productive scholar addressing a great range of topics, many of which we have not been able to consider in this book.

Further, in recent years it seems that we cannot attend a conference presentation or read a scholarly article without finding ourselves considering the role that interbehavioral thinking could play in such circumstances as overcoming conflicts, understanding foundations, facilitating interdisciplinary relations, developing more comprehensive applications to socially important issues, and more. And while it might not be surprising that we, as committed interbehaviorists, would find interbehaviorism to be relevant to these many things, it seems that we are not alone. All of this is to say that we're not writing this book now just because introductory books on Kantor's work are scarce, but also because it seems like the time is right for this book.

We don't think the growing interest in interbehaviorism is due to problems or missteps in what has been going on in behavior science. Quite the opposite. In our view, the growing interest in interbehaviorism is likely a result of the progress of behavior science. For example, our understanding of linguistic behavior has become more elaborate in recent years (Fryling, Rehfeldt, Tarbox, & Hayes, 2020). We've also found it necessary to reconsider things that seemed settled, such as reinforcement theory. In our view, these and other changes and developments are pushing us toward a more interbehavioral way of thinking.

How This Book Is Organized

This book is organized into two general parts. Part 1, Foundations, starts with topics pertinent to J.R. Kantor's philosophy of science, interbehaviorism (chapters 1 and 2). After reviewing these philosophical foundations, we provide an overview of the central themes of interbehavioral psychology (chapter 3). Part 1 also includes chapters on investigation (chapter 4) and application (chapter 5). Part 2 of the text, Theoretical Applications, builds upon part 1 by focusing on extensions of interbehavioral thinking to important areas of research and practice, including linguistic behavior, memory, perspective-taking and relationships, feelings, human development, family values, and morality. Part 2 in particular builds upon Kantor's analysis of stimulus substitution and implicit behavior. These processes are especially relevant to an understanding of complex events as are considered in part 2 of the book. Words that appear in **bold** are further defined in the glossary at the back of the book.

Part I

Foundations

This first part of the book focuses on the foundations of the interbehavioral perspective on philosophy and science. In the early chapters, especially 1 and 2, we review information pertinent to **interbehaviorism** as a philosophy of science. This content is fundamental, pertaining to the interbehavioral perspective on all scientific activity, including that in the discipline of psychology. The analyses provided throughout the entire text are based upon the material reviewed in these first two chapters. Topics in these initial two chapters include the definition of science, **disciplinary science** and **interdisciplinary science,** scientific constructs, and assumptions and their role in scientific disciplines, among others. Chapter 2 gives special attention to **scientific systems** and includes information related to the subsystems of scientific disciplines.

Chapter 3 begins our specific focus on the discipline of psychology and involves an overview of the assumptions upon which the discipline is constructed. These assumptions address issues such as causality, the relationship of psychology to other sciences, and the multifactored nature of the subject matter, among others. Importantly, the interbehavioral field construct is introduced in this chapter, which is central to the interbehavioral analysis of psychological happenings.

Chapter 4 turns to the topic of research and addresses conceptual, methodological, and other issues pertaining to the investigative subsystem of psychology. Perennial problems in the research domain are addressed, including a discussion of the nature and value of research. The interbehavioral perspective is further clarified through a description of how interbehavioral research may be pursued in different areas. Throughout all of these examples, we emphasize the value of the interbehavioral perspective in promoting a more comprehensive understanding of difficult issues.

The applied subsystem of the science of psychology is the focus of chapter 5. In this chapter, we discuss common areas of practice and analyze them from an interbehavioral perspective. The interbehavioral approach is presented as an alternative to a number of common practices in the field of behavior analysis and psychology more generally.

CHAPTER 1

Science and Philosophy

We begin with a consideration of Kantor's approach to the philosophy of science and to his particular philosophical system, interbehaviorism. We start here because Kantor's psychological system is built upon the philosophical foundation expressed as interbehaviorism. In Kantor's view, while all of the sciences have their foundations in agreed-upon definitions of and premises concerning their unique subject matters, individual scientists may not be fully aware of these foundations or their value in the scientific domain. To fortify the notion that philosophy requires consideration in its own right and to build a solid foundation upon which to pursue a comprehensive science of psychology, interbehaviorism is laid out in thorough and explicit detail at multiple levels of scope.

We begin with Kantor's analysis of science in general and ask the question "What is science?" (Kantor, 1953, p.3). From this general consideration of scientific work will follow a discussion of disciplinary and interdisciplinary science, and how these two types of science may be conceptualized from an interbehavioral perspective. After this, we describe the aims of natural sciences and how they differ from the aims of other types of human enterprise. The chapter concludes with an overview of how a valid philosophy of science may be developed and includes consideration of the distinction between constructs and events. Finally, we will preview topics to be addressed in the next chapter. We now turn to our first topic and attempt to answer the question "What is science?" from an interbehavioral perspective.

What Is Science?

In his 1953 text, Kantor approached the identity of science by adopting an observational procedure to describe it. In other words, Kantor suggested that we might discover what science is by observing scientists at work. This involved an examination of the various factors involved in scientific work, including the scientific worker, the work, the things worked with, the tools and instruments employed, the circumstances under which the work is conducted, and the products of the work as it is completed (Kantor, 1953, pp.8–9). This may seem simple enough, but adopting this observational approach involves acknowledging some important philosophical issues. To start, in taking this approach it becomes obvious that science is not a means of achieving universal and absolute laws. The scope of science is much more limited than the whole of the universe, and the products of science are not stable enough to be absolute. In other words, science is not and cannot be about achieving a universal understanding that applies to everything, nor is scientific knowledge ever final or complete. Science is a much more humble, human activity when viewed in this way (this has implications for other issues to be addressed in subsequent chapters). And, while science is neither universal nor absolute, it is also not merely a method of discovery or investigation (Kantor, 1953, p.4). Indeed, science also involves theory, the products of investigation, and more (more on this in chapter 2).

Given this, Kantor (1953, p.4) suggested that "what science is can only be determined on the basis of the unique activities involved in determining: a) the existence of certain things and events and b) the characteristics of such things when they do exist." We might say that science is about discovering certain things and events and understanding the features of those events once we discover them. In our view, the science of psychology is likely to focus on the latter; more on this in coming chapters. Following from this, science "turns out to be an enormous accumulation of specific jobs" (Kantor, 1953, p.4); the jobs, as such, are all aimed at affording a continuously evolving orientation toward existing things and events. This is to say, all of the jobs involved in science as a whole are aspects of the larger effort to learn more and more about the world. This learning involves a) repeated confrontations with the events we are interested in while considering the knowledge already accumulated about those events to the present point and b) approaching those events in new ways. These two factors serve to distinguish scientific work from other types of work. In sum, science is a serious enterprise and its outcomes, if successful, are novel. Other types of work lack one or both of these features (Kantor, 1953, pp.6–7).

Importantly, this perspective on what science is also suggests that there may be multiple sciences, each addressing a unique subject matter with tools and instruments suited to it. Given this, we now consider the nature of disciplinary and interdisciplinary sciences, and provide an overview of our perspective on these issues (as described at length in Hayes & Fryling, 2009b).

Disciplinary and Interdisciplinary Sciences

There are many reasons to consider the unique features of both disciplinary and interdisciplinary sciences, and Kantor's work contributes to a better understanding of both types of scientific endeavors, including the relationships between them. These issues are elaborated upon in this section.

Disciplinary Science

As we have described thus far, science may be considered an accumulation of scientific jobs. While scientists may share a general interest in learning about the world of nature, and that world may be considered one integrated whole, it is not the case that any scientist actually studies the entirety of the world of nature. No scientist can study everything, in other words. Indeed, the matrix of natural happenings comprising the world of nature is too large and complex to be subject to any one scientific effort. For this reason, scientists tend to focus on a particular aspect of the matrix of natural happenings to identify and focus on a specific subject matter. Importantly, this isn't because those subject matters exist as independent entities out there in the world of nature. Rather, the things studied by biologists and physicists, for example, are isolated from the world of nature by an arbitrary procedure and constructed as unique subject matters by which the disciplines of biology and physics are distinguished as different disciplinary sciences. The events studied by biologists and physicists are not independent of each other. This is to say, the world of nature does not exist in parts. However, the verbal isolation of different event types and their construction as unique subject matters permits scientists to focus on less than the whole world of nature. In other words, the fact that unique subject matters are constructed permits the development and continuation of disciplinary sciences.

We find this point to be especially central to understanding interbehavioral thinking on these issues. It means that specific attention needs to be given to the subject matter of any particular disciplinary science, including how it is related to neighboring sciences and more (we will elaborate on some of these issues in chapters 2 and 3). As far as our consideration of disciplinary sciences go, though, we note that the identification of unique subject matters has implications for the value of such sciences. The productivity of a disciplinary science depends in large part on its continued focus on a particular subject matter. This is the case because when scientists of a particular **collectivity** are organized around and focused upon a particular set of events, the outcomes of investigation more readily accumulate as a coherent body of knowledge on the topic of interest. Further, as this particular set of events is not the focus of any other scientific discipline, the contributions of a disciplinary science are unique and are thereby uniquely valuable to the overall accumulation of scientific knowledge (Hayes & Fryling, 2015).

Raised by our consideration of disciplinary sciences is another point that has bearing on our upcoming conceptualization of interdisciplinary sciences. Recall that the subject matters of all disciplinary sciences are arbitrarily constructed and derived from the world of natural happenings. The fact that the subject matters of all of the disciplinary sciences are derived from the same matrix of natural happenings, and that they are arbitrarily constructed, underscores the fact that the subject matters of all of the disciplinary sciences are of equal status. That is, no subject matter is held to be more important, more basic, or more fundamental than any other; further, no subject matter is held to be required for the existence of the subject matter of another (Observer, 1969). Note that this supposition is at odds with more traditional thinking, where **psychological events** are held to be enacted by, exist as, or be caused by biological events, particularly neurological events. From an interbehavioral perspective, the subject matter of one scientific discipline doesn't cause the subject matter of another discipline to occur. Again, all of the sciences have equal status in the scientific domain, none more important or more influential than any of the others.

All of this is to say that disciplinary sciences are organized around understanding a specific set of events, derived from the larger matrix of natural happenings. The focus on this subject matter facilitates the accumulation of knowledge about such events. Still, disciplinary sciences are one thing, interdisciplinary sciences are another.

As mentioned previously, our consideration of disciplinary sciences has implications for how we construct interdisciplinary sciences. We begin by describing an interbehavioral approach to the conceptualization of interdisciplinary sciences, followed by a consideration of problematic conceptualizations of interdisciplinary science.

Interdisciplinary Sciences

Interdisciplinary sciences are both similar and dissimilar to disciplinary sciences. Like disciplinary sciences, interdisciplinary sciences are tasked with identifying a unique subject matter so as to make a contribution to the larger body of scientific knowledge. Unlike disciplinary sciences, though, the subject matters of interdisciplinary sciences are *not* derived from that matrix of natural happenings. Rather, the subject matters of interdisciplinary sciences consist of relations among the subject matters of participating disciplinary sciences. Figure 1.1 depicts the differences between the subject matters of disciplinary and interdisciplinary sciences. The example of psychology is provided for the disciplinary science subject matter. Here, *sf* refers to **stimulus function,** and *rf* refers to **response function** (this is considered in more detail in chapter 3).

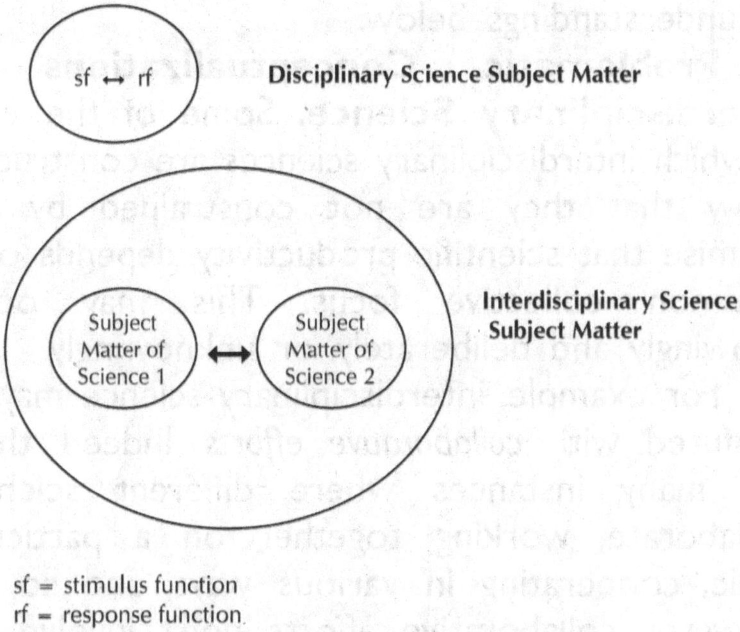

Figure 1.1. Disciplinary vs. Interdisciplinary Science

This conceptualization of the subject matters of interdisciplinary sciences is in keeping with our contention that by identifying and focusing upon something unique, a science may contribute to the accumulation of knowledge undertaken by the sciences at large. A failure to appreciate the value of a science in these terms has resulted in several problematic conceptualizations of interdisciplinary science. That is, a failure to appreciate the unique features of, and therefore the boundaries of, disciplinary sciences leads to misunderstandings as to the nature of interdisciplinary sciences. We elaborate on these misunderstandings below.

Problematic Conceptualizations of Interdisciplinary Science. Some of the ways in which interdisciplinary sciences are constructed show that they are not constrained by the premise that scientific productivity depends on a common collective focus. This may occur knowingly and deliberately, or unknowingly.

For example, interdisciplinary science may be confused with *collaborative efforts*. Indeed, there are many instances where different sciences collaborate, working together on a particular topic, cooperating in various ways, and so on. However, collaborative efforts don't involve the study of something *new*, as is the requirement for both a valid disciplinary and a valid interdisciplinary science from an interbehavioral perspective. Rather, the collaborating disciplines are more or less working in parallel here, and the work resulting from such collaborative efforts may contribute to an understanding of the subject matters of one or more of the collaborating sciences. However, unless the work contributes to the understanding of a new subject matter—the unique subject matter of the interdisciplinary science—collaboration does not constitute an interdisciplinary science, as nothing new is investigated.

Other times an interdisciplinary science is held to be achieved by the practice of rearranging or disregarding the boundary conditions of the participating disciplinary sciences. This may be done deliberately or occur unknowingly. Nonetheless, overlooking scientific boundary conditions does not render the practice of doing so an interdisciplinary science. In fact, the result may not even be a contribution to an understanding of the subject matters of the participating disciplinary sciences, as it may detract from the focus of both disciplines. For example, oftentimes boundary conditions are deliberately rearranged when psychology collaborates with biology, with the data resulting from such work being entirely biological in nature. This is an outcome of reductionistic ideas that biology underlies psychology. Similarly, the science of psychology may attempt to study cultural issues by rearranging its disciplinary focus to include the behavior of groups. The results of such practices are likely to be expressed in psychological terminology or in sociological terminology, but not in terms of a new subject matter that neither has isolated as its own.

Problematic conceptualizations of interdisciplinary science also occur when the products of one scientific discipline are used in another—for example, when concepts derived from the study of individuals in highly restricted contexts are then applied to the analysis of groups. It is important to note that many of these examples are related to a more general misunderstanding of disciplinary sciences themselves. That is, if there isn't an understanding of the requirement that valid disciplinary sciences must identify and focus upon a unique subject matter, then interdisciplinary sciences are likely to be constructed on faulty premises from the outset. Readers interested in a more thorough treatment of these issues may consult Hayes and Fryling (2009b).

Still, there is something even more fundamental needing our attention here. Interbehaviorism takes a natural science approach, and this natural science approach is the foundation for everything from an interbehavioral perspective.

A Natural Science of Behavior

One of the most important features of interbehavioral philosophy is its focus on the development of the natural sciences. This includes work in the philosophy of science, all of the disciplinary sciences, and more. To begin, we should consider what a natural science amounts to and how it is distinguished from other ways of approaching science. The natural sciences are focused on the confrontable world of nature. Implied by this is the assumption that the natural world is all there is to study. In other words, it isn't the case that there is a world of nature that can be studied and "another world" that can't. Ideas of two worlds, one natural and one supernatural, are incompatible with the aims of scientific activity. While all of the behaviorisms embrace this premise of natural science, interbehaviorism is especially consistent in its commitment to the aims of natural sciences. Adhering to natural science aims appears to be especially difficult when the subject of analysis is human behavior. The following section addresses some of these complications.

Science and Culture

Earlier in this chapter we attempted to answer the question "What is science?" In doing so, we highlighted the fact that what science is can only be determined by studying what scientists do. In other words, science is a job that people engage in. This view of science seems to draw attention to the scientific worker more than other ways of conceptualizing science may. Indeed, the scientist is an active participant in what happens in the work of science. Acknowledging the participation of the scientist in the practices and outcomes of scientific work is central to understanding the challenge of committing to natural science aims in the analysis of human behavior.

Kantor elaborates on these issues in his text *The Logic of Modern Science* (Kantor, 1953, pp.26–28). Here Kantor draws attention to the undeniable fact that scientists are people, people who were raised and continue to live in collectivities composed of persons with whom they share histories. While this may seem obvious, it is in ordinary communities that dualistic folklore is rampant, and it is not possible for members of these communities to fully abandon their histories of dualistic indoctrination even once they have become natural scientists.

Dualistic ideas permeate our ways of speaking and thinking about everything, and this means that the work of scientists is certain to be influenced by these ideas, at least to some degree. This is to say, scientists are not *immune* to nonscientific ways of thinking merely because they are scientists by occupation. For this reason, Kantor calls for philosophers of science to continuously assess the work of scientists, to evaluate the extent to which the work of science is derived from contacts with events relative to the cultural context more generally. Kantor goes on to suggest that the work of the philosopher of science is itself scientific work, its subject matter being the products of scientists' linguistic behavior. That is, the descriptive and explanatory constructions developed by scientists as they encounter features of the world of nature become the subject matter of the science of philosophy. Figure 1.2 depicts the interactions of the scientist and their subject matter. In this example, the subject matter is again that of the science of psychology, with *sf* referring to **stimulus function** and *rf* referring to **response function.** The cultural context is also represented here.

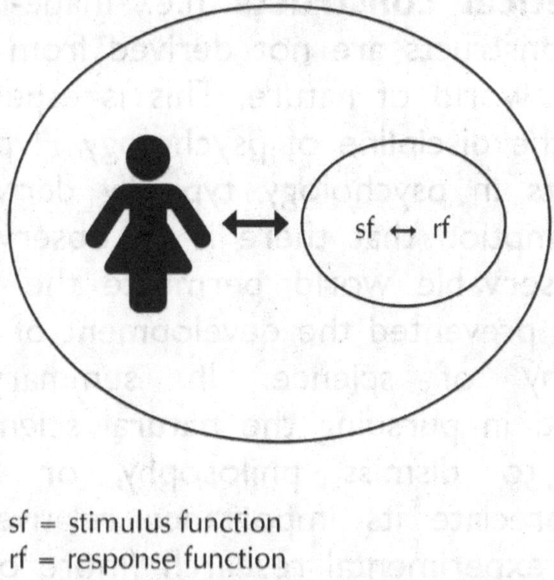

Figure 1.2. Science and Culture

Developing a Natural Philosophy of Science

We consider at this point how a natural science of philosophy is developed and sustained. To many people, including scientists, philosophy is seen as something distinct from science—the idea is that "there is philosophy and then there is *science*." Worse, philosophy may even be viewed as something "made up," consisting of nothing more than what someone thinks about something, more or less, and nothing more. This view that philosophy is one thing, science another, comes from people's experience with philosophies articulated as collections of

hypothetical constructs (i.e., made-up stuff). These constructs are not derived from contacts with the world of nature. This is especially the case in the discipline of psychology. Hypothetical constructs in psychology, typically derived from the assumption that there is an observable and an unobservable world, permeate the discipline and have prevented the development of a natural philosophy of science. In summary, many interested in pursuing the natural sciences have learned to dismiss philosophy, or at best, underappreciate its importance relative to the value of experimental research (more on this in chapter 3).

Kantor's approach to the philosophy of science is aligned with the natural science aims of all interbehavioral thinking. To start, it is important to acknowledge that philosophical work is uniquely constructed from an interbehavioral perspective. In this regard, Kantor (1969) distinguishes between **valid philosophy** and **invalid philosophy.** Invalid philosophy is founded on premises that are not derived from contacts with the natural world. On the contrary, invalid philosophy is founded upon dualistic ideas and cultural folklore. Invalid philosophies are what gives philosophy the reputation that it is irrelevant to science. Valid philosophy is distinguished from invalid philosophy in that the premises involved in valid philosophies *are* derived from contacts with events in the natural world. When this is the basis for philosophical work, that work may indeed be of service to the work of scientists, particularly those interested in developing a natural science of psychology. Moreover, philosophical work, like all scientific work, is considered to be ongoing and evolving, constantly building upon previous work. The work involved in maintaining and improving upon the foundation of work in the philosophy of science is the topic of the next chapter.

We conclude this chapter by introducing a distinction that is of central importance to interbehavioral philosophy, and something to which we have been alluding but have not yet directly addressed. This is the distinction between constructs and events as outlined by Kantor (e.g., 1957).

Constructs and Events

Interbehavioral thinking places special emphasis on the distinction between constructs and events (e.g., Kantor, 1957). Generally, this distinction refers to the difference between the events we are interested in studying and what we *say* about those events. This is the distinction between the subject matter of the science of psychology and the terms we use to describe, investigate, and interpret that subject matter. The distinction between constructs and events is important because oftentimes, both within the science of psychology and the sciences more generally, constructs are *confused with events*. In other words, there is a tendency for scientists to confuse the way in which they describe, investigate, and interpret their subject matter with that subject matter itself.

A number of problems may emerge from this confusion. The problem of confusing constructs with events is especially likely in the science of psychology, where the subject matter has a number of features that may promote the confusion (Fryling & Hayes, 2009). We describe some of these features and examples of confusions between constructs and events more in chapter 3, which focuses on the subject matter of psychology.

We have noted several areas where the confusion between constructs and events has resulted in philosophical confusion (e.g., Hayes et al., 1997), theoretical debate (e.g., Fryling, 2013a; Hayes, 1992a), and more, with the result that investigations are pursued and interpreted from problematic foundations (e.g., Fryling, 2017). Given that the distinction between constructs and events is not fully recognized and appreciated within the various areas of behavior science, we suspect that there are countless examples where constructs are confused with events. We introduce the distinction here because it is fundamental to interbehavioral philosophy, as well as to many other topics from an interbehavioral perspective.

Summary and Key Points

This chapter provided a brief overview of some of the fundamental features of interbehavioral philosophy. This included a consideration of what science is and is not, as well as an overview of both disciplinary and interdisciplinary science from an interbehavioral perspective. Following this, we discussed the value of having a natural science perspective. Within that discussion, we considered the way in which culture influences science, as well as what constitutes a valid philosophy of science. The chapter concluded with a description of the distinction between constructs and events from an interbehavioral perspective. While most of the content of the present chapter is foundational in nature, the next chapter delves into more detail on the topic of interbehavioral philosophy, including how scientific systems are organized and evaluated from an interbehavioral perspective.

Study Questions

1. How does Kantor suggest we go about answering the question "What is science?" What are the implications of this?

2. What does it mean that the subject matters are arbitrarily constructed? How does this relate to sciences having equal status?

3. How are the subject matters of interdisciplinary sciences both similar to and

different from the subject matters of disciplinary sciences?

4. Explain two problematic conceptualizations of interdisciplinary sciences.

5. Why is the relationship between science and culture especially important when considering natural science aims?

6. How do hypothetical constructs relate to Kantor's distinction between valid and invalid philosophies?

7. Describe the distinction between constructs and events using an example.

CHAPTER 2

Psychology as a Scientific System

In the previous chapter we described some of the main features of interbehaviorism as a philosophy of science. These features highlight the most important philosophical assumptions of interbehaviorism, and more generally underscore the extent to which interbehaviorism views philosophy as a scientific discipline in its own right. That is, to interbehaviorism, the philosophy of science isn't just a "sideshow" to everything else. The philosophy of science has its own unique subject matter, which includes studying the extent to which the products of science are influenced by both contacts with events (i.e., interactions with the world) and cultural folklore (i.e., nonscientific ideas in the culture). The fact that the philosophy of science is a distinct science in its own right also means that, like all sciences, it is neither absolute nor universal (Kantor, 1953). This means that the philosophy of science will never reach an ultimate ending, nor will an understanding one day be achieved that may apply to everything. Philosophy too is always evolving. Exactly how sciences go about evolving, how they go about continuous self-improvement and evaluation, is another issue.

This chapter focuses on scientific systems specifically. The word "system" is used in a couple of interrelated ways within interbehavioral thinking, both to describe **system building** and to refer to scientific disciplines being constructed as systems themselves. That is, scientific disciplines are **scientific systems.** We begin the chapter by describing system building and then explore scientific systems.

System Building

As we described in the previous chapter, interbehaviorism highlights the extent to which cultural folklore (e.g., especially commonsense dualism) influences everything we do. Mentalistic ideas, including all of their many problems, permeate our entire world. Moreover, scientists, as people who are also living in this world, simply can't escape it. For this reason, it is important for scientists to make clear their assumptions about the world, their aims, how these relate to conducting research, how they are applied to socially important issues, and more. The pervasiveness of nonscientific ideas throughout the world requires us to give this careful attention. We need to do more than just *say* we are objective or that we take a "scientific approach" to things. Indeed, failing to give very specific attention to these issues only ensures that they will remain present.

It isn't just that we have nonscientific ideas to worry about, especially in psychological science; there are many other important issues that warrant attention in the discipline. We often struggle to know exactly what we're studying, for example. Not being clear about something as fundamental as what we are studying has serious implications, too. For example, lack of clarity surrounding this issue impacts how we do research, and of course, how we do research ultimately impacts how we practice in clinical settings (more on this in chapters 4 and 5). The lack of clarity regarding what we are studying also impacts our relationships with other sciences—and indeed, it isn't always clear how psychological science relates to other disciplines, especially those that are close "neighbors" (e.g., biology). This issue is important given that the measurement of biological and neurological happenings has become more widespread in science. It's interesting that these sorts of issues, while they seem to impact everything we do, don't often get very much attention. For the most part we seem to ignore these issues and carry on.

Neglecting these issues will take us only so far. Worse, it may lead to our efforts being fragmented and disorganized, and to our failing to build upon our progress (Fryling & Hayes, 2009). Something more is required; specific efforts are needed to organize sciences to maximize their progress.

In interbehaviorism, these efforts are described as system building. System building describes the organizing activity involved in articulating philosophical assumptions about various areas of a scientific discipline. In describing the importance of system construction, Kantor (1958, p.48) writes, "This organizing activity (a) helps to make clear the kind of things and events dealt with, (b) brings into relief the boundaries of specific scientific domains and their relations to other departments of science, and (c) facilitates an examination of assumptions and procedures employed." Here, Kantor is describing how system building helps us identify the specific aspects of the subject matter that we are focusing on (i.e., exactly what we are studying), understand how psychological science relates to other sciences, and evaluate our assumptions, research methods, and more. Kantor (1958, p.50) describes some broad aims of system building and some guiding principles.

Validity and Significance

The most basic principles guiding system building pertain to the concepts of **validity** and **significance.** While these terms are familiar in psychology and the helping professions (e.g., they are common in assessment and research methods literature), they are used somewhat differently in the context of system building as understood here. **Validity** refers to internal consistency within system building efforts (Kantor, 1958). In other words, validity pertains to the extent to which a scientific system is internally consistent. We might say that validity asks the question "Is the system free from contradictions?" A number of questions follow from this, such as "Is work occurring in one area aligned with work in another area?" and "Is the way we interpret our research at odds with our philosophical assumptions?" System building efforts focus on assessing scientific systems to identify various areas where validity may be improved upon, and ideally, provide a means by which validity might be achieved.

Significance is similar to validity in the sense that it refers to a lack of contradiction. However, in the case of significance, the consistency is with respect to other sciences (Kantor, 1958). In other words, significance asks the question "How consistent are the premises of one science with those of another science and the family of sciences more generally?" A psychological system could be internally consistent (e.g., a thorough psychoanalytic formulation) but be inconsistent with the premises of the larger family of sciences (e.g., biology, chemistry, physics). Importantly, validity is a prerequisite to significance. This is to say, if a science isn't internally consistent, if it isn't free from contradiction within itself, then it is not possible to assess the extent to which it is consistent with other sciences.

Comprehensiveness

In addition to matters of validity and significance, the **comprehensiveness** of a scientific system must be taken into consideration. A scientific system may be both valid and significant yet fail to account for the full range of happenings that fall within its purview. For example, the system of behavior analysis has examined the basic principles involved in countless research studies, assessment protocols, and intervention programs. The question of comprehensiveness asks, "How well do those principles and processes account for all behavior?" As some readers of this book may be aware, theoretical developments in the area of verbal behavior (or more broadly, language and cognition) pertain to this topic. The authors have attempted to articulate how the science of behavior could improve upon its comprehensiveness in a manner that promotes both validity and significance. The second part of this text is dedicated to such issues. Our point in addressing the topic of comprehensiveness here is that while validity and significance are important evaluative measures, the comprehensiveness of a science must also be considered. Moreover, from our perspective, a lack of comprehensiveness is connected to issues of validity (and by extension, significance).

Our key points so far: 1) Scientific disciplines, especially those that aim to be a part of the family of natural sciences, must make deliberate attempts to organize and evaluate themselves. From an interbehavioral perspective, this is accomplished by system building. 2) Scientific systems must strive toward both validity and significance, the former being a prerequisite for the latter, while also taking into consideration the comprehensiveness of the science.

The Pyramid

Figure 2.1 depicts Kantor's "Ziggurat of Science" (adapted from Kantor & Smith, 1975, p.410), which we will refer to as "the pyramid" for our purposes. The pyramid provides a visual representation of some of the issues we have described thus far.

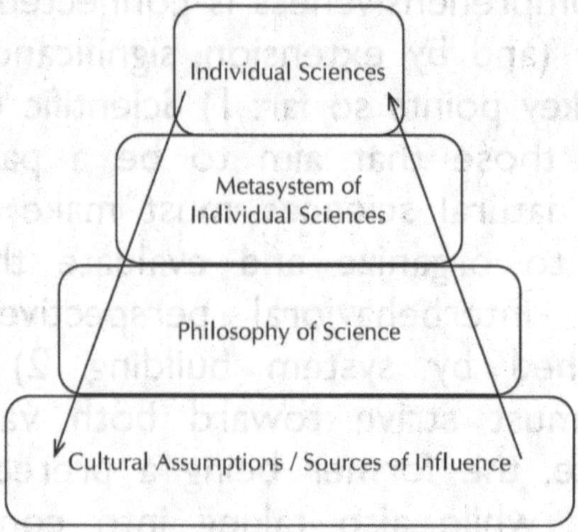

Figure 2.1. Ziggurat of Science and Civilization

Cultural Matrix

At the bottom of the pyramid is the "cultural matrix," which represents the wide range of assumptions, ideas, and beliefs that permeate all of society. As previously mentioned, interbehaviorism is unique in the sense that it specifically calls attention to the presence of these factors in everything that scientists do—there is no escaping the fact that scientific work is conducted by people who are at the same time participating in a larger cultural context. The same goes for therapists and helping professionals. They too are members of a cultural collectivity that includes long-standing ideas about human behavior. There is simply no removing the challenge posed by the cultural matrix. What we can do is be aware of it and examine the extent to which it influences our work.

Philosophy of Science

The next level of the pyramid pertains to the premises of the philosophy of science, many of which were touched upon in the previous chapter. It is noteworthy that interbehaviorism specifically articulates these assumptions. We know of no other system of contemporary psychology that does so. Table 2.1 lists these assumptions as they are addressed in Kantor's writings (see Kantor, 1958, pp.70–71; Kantor & Smith, 1975, pp.412–13).

Table 2.1. Assumptions of the Philosophy of Science in Interbehaviorism

1	Science is the enterprise of interbehaving with specific things and events that leads to a definite and precise orientation with respect to those things and events.
2	Scientific orientation concerns a) the existence and identity of things and events and their components and b) the relationship between either the components of things and events, or between the various things and events themselves.
3	No science is concerned with existences or processes that transcend the boundaries of scientific enterprises. No scientific problem is concerned with a "reality" beyond confrontable events and their investigation.
4	Scientific orientation requires specialized instruments and methods depending upon a) the specific characteristics of the events interacted with and b) the specific problems formulated about them.

5	Scientific interactions eventuate in protocols (records), hypotheses, theories, and laws.
6	Scientific construction—the formulation of a) hypotheses and b) theories and laws—must be derived from interbehavior with events and not imposed upon the events or scientific enterprise from nonscientific cultural sources.
7	Culture consists of the events and institutions (religion, art, economics, technology, social organization, and laws) of a specific group of people.
8	Scientific enterprises are evolutional; they develop in cultural situations as complex institutions. Scientific domains are cumulative and corrigible. They are completely free from all absolutes, ultimates, or universals.
9	Scientific enterprises can be and sometimes are autonomous and fundamental within a cultural complex. Only specific enterprises may cooperate and mutually influence each other with respect to basic investigational and interpretive procedures.
10	Applications of a) scientific findings (records concerning events and their investigation) and b) investigative results (laws and theories) may be localized within scientific enterprises. Such applications constitute the authentic basis for scientific prediction and control.

Metasystem of Psychology

Just above the assumptions pertaining to the philosophy of science are those of the metasystem of psychology. Kantor refers to these assumptions as **postulates.** They address psychological science in particular, focusing on broad issues pertaining to the discipline and its relations with other sciences. We provide an overview of the postulates of the metasystem as they are described in Kantor's writings below (Kantor, 1958, pp.65–68; Kantor & Smith, 1975, pp.413–15), and have also included a table that provides a translation in lay terms (table 2.2).

Postulate 1: Psychology is homogeneous with all other sciences. All scientific disciplines have the aim of understanding their unique subject matters, all of which are derived from the same matrix of happenings that comprise the natural world. In Kantor's words, "Each science, including psychology, isolates some phase of this manifold for its special object of study" (1958, p.65). While all sciences are similar in their focus on a subject matter derived from the matrix of natural happenings, they differ in their specific methods as required by the features of their subject matter. In this sense, all sciences are natural sciences, and as Kantor suggests, if there is to be any hierarchy among them it should be based on their relative accomplishments (1958, p.66).

Postulate 2: Psychology is a relatively independent science. As just described, all of the sciences are derived from the same matrix of natural happenings. While this is something that makes all of the sciences similar, they are still relatively independent of one another. Each science, including the science of psychology, develops its own body of knowledge pertaining to its unique subject matter. As such, the findings and constructs of one science cannot be borrowed or used to explain the subject matter of another science.

Importantly, the subject matters of some scientific disciplines are more closely related than others, and the scientists involved in those disciplines may study those subject matters in similar ways. For example, psychology and biology are more closely related than psychology and geology. Regardless, psychology is a unique science and does not need another science to validate its findings. In Kantor's words, "Psychology, then, does not require any specific neural or general biological guarantee for the authenticity of its data" (1958, p.66). In summary, while some sciences may be more or less closely related than others, they always maintain their unique area of focus and therefore remain relatively independent.

Postulate 3: An interbehavioral system of psychology departs from all traditional epistemological and ontological systems. As we have discussed, a natural science of psychology must dissociate from all traditional philosophical assumptions concerning its subject matter. This includes a complete departure from all dualistic philosophies.

Postulate 4: A psychological system should achieve a comprehensive coverage of events, operations, and theory constructions. An adequate science of psychology must address the full range of happenings that fall within the scope of its subject matter. In other words, a science of psychology cannot restrict its purview to a narrow range of relatively simple events to the exclusion of more complex aspects of its subject matter. Kantor (e.g., 1970) suggests that the neglect of complex events is exemplified when psychologists are overly focused on learning, as has occurred in behavior analysis. Part 2 of this text attempts to rectify this circumstance.

Postulate 5: System construction requires adequate orientation with respect to systemological problems. This postulate describes the importance of having familiarity with system building and an orientation to scientific disciplines as scientific systems. This means that scientists must do more than simply acknowledge the value of system building, but also understand how to pursue system building activities in the ongoing pursuit of a natural science of psychology. Indeed, scientists must be watchful of system problems and how they may be solved. As we have mentioned in this chapter, a failure to be oriented to system building and its related issues ensures that dualistic ideas will continue to flourish.

Postulate 6: A psychological system is not reducible to any other type. This assumption addresses a long-standing assumption that the subject matters of some sciences may be reduced to the subject matters of other sciences—for example, that psychology may be reduced to biology. Kantor asks, "Is any science basic to any other? Is mathematics basic to physics, physics to biology, biology to psychology? Those who say 'yes' we classify as reductionists" (Kantor, 1958, p.68). Psychology, being a science like all of the others in the sense that it has isolated a unique subject matter derived from the larger matrix of natural happenings, cannot be reduced to the subject matter of any other science. There is no hierarchy among the natural sciences.

Postulate 7: Psychological systems are relative and subject to continual corrective reformulation. There are no universals or absolutes in science. As such, the science of psychology is in a state of constant self-correction, always changing and building upon previous systemic findings in all aspects of the system.

Individual Sciences

Finally, at the top of the pyramid are assumptions, or premises, pertaining to specific disciplinary formulations—in our case, the assumptions pertain to the system of interbehavioral psychology. These premises will be discussed in more detail in chapter 3. where our focus is on interbehavioral psychology in particular.

Table 2.2. Sample Philosophical Premises Pertaining to the Metasystem of Interbehavioral Psychology

Original Language	Translation
Psychology is homogeneous with all other sciences.	Psychology is a science like all of the other sciences.
Psychology is a relatively independent science.	Psychology is a unique science.
An interbehavioral system of psychology departs from all traditional epistemological and ontological systems.	Interbehavioral psychology drops all traditions of dualism, reductionism, absolutism, and so on.
A psychological system should achieve a comprehensive coverage of events, operations, and theory constructions.	Psychology should strive to be complete and cover all topics relevant to the discipline.
System construction requires adequate orientation with respect to systemological problems.	Developing a disciplinary system requires one to understand systems.
A psychological system is not reducible to any other type.	Psychology cannot be reduced to any other science. It is valid on its own.
Psychological systems are relative and subject to continual corrective reformulation.	Psychological science is always evolving, updating, and revising.

Tasks of the System Builder

System building is an area of work that involves specific tasks. While a number of tasks might fall within the work of system building as we have described it thus far, Kantor (1969) describes three specific tasks that we will outline here. They include monitorial, semantic supervision, and coordination. The **monitorial task** of the system builder pertains to how different assumptions and terms are developed and employed within the scientific discipline. In the previous chapter we drew attention to the important distinction between constructs and events. The monitorial task with respect to this issue involves evaluating the extent to which different assumptions, terms, and practices within a system are derived from contacts with the natural environment as opposed to cultural tradition (see chapter 1 regarding this). This task is of utmost importance from an interbehavioral perspective given its commitment to the development of a natural science of psychology. System building tasks of the **semantic supervision** sort involve the system builder assessing and evaluating how terms are used within the discipline. Terms may be used inconsistently, they may be derived from other disciplines where they have other meanings, or they may carry traditional folklore with them (e.g., see Fryling & Hayes, 2011 on the term "function" in behavior analysis). Finally, the third task of system building is **coordination** of the findings and interpretations of the various disciplinary sciences so as to eliminate contradictions among them.

Thus far we have talked about systems in the context of system building, and how systems are continuously evaluated and develop as natural sciences. This final section of the chapter focuses on sciences as systems themselves. We use the science of psychology as an example.

The Science of Psychology as a Scientific System

Interbehavioral thinking views scientific disciplines as scientific systems. While all scientific disciplines could be conceptualized in this way, Kantor was specifically focused on developing the science of psychology as a scientific system, and his 1958 text, *Interbehavioral Psychology: A Sample of Scientific System Construction,* was dedicated to that task. We provide an overview of some of the key points of Kantor's analysis in this section.

The conceptualization and construction of a scientific discipline as a system draws attention to the fact that different parts of scientific work—its basic and applied parts, for example—comprise an integrated whole. The parts, as such, are related to one another and none is more important than any other.

As just alluded to, systems have parts, which Kantor refers to as subsystems. In psychological systems, these include investigative, interpretive, and applied subsystems. To many in behavior science, these areas are better known as research, theory, and application and/or practice. While these subsystems have their own unique areas of focus, they remain parts of the larger whole. Implied here is that at no time is a subsystem to be confused with the entire system of psychology. Chapter 4 focuses on the investigative system. Here we focus briefly on the applied and interpretive subsystems, beginning with the former.

The Applied Subsystem

The applied subsystem is home to the majority of the work within psychological science. In addition to this distinguishing factor, the applied subsystem is unique because it is "intimately related to practical manipulation" (Kantor, 1958, p.157). As a result, pragmatic concerns exert considerably more influence over the work in the applied subsystem than in the other subsystems. For example, research aimed at producing a clinical outcome faster or with less professional involvement seems to be especially influenced by practical, nonscientific circumstances (Fryling, 2011). In addition to this, various areas of the applied subsystem may have little to do with each other. For example, applied research focused on teaching language to individuals with language delays may have little to do with research focused on organizational behavior, which may have little to do with research on psychotherapy processes and outcomes.

The applied subsystem, optimally, serves the purpose of verification according to Kantor (1958, pp.57–58). That is, from Kantor's perspective, the aim of research in the applied subsystem is to verify that the findings achieved in laboratory analog arrangements are applicable to behavior occurring in real-world circumstances. When research in the applied subsystem progresses in this way, it is discovery oriented, as new information is obtained. This new information may then result in revisions of interpretations pertaining to the topic, set the stage for additional investigations, and so on. In this sense, the verification function of the applied subsystem contributes to the progress of the disciplinary system more generally. By contrast, the applied subsystem is exploited when practical circumstances overshadow scientific aims. In Kantor's words, "Hardly avoidable is the extreme situation in which the utility motive dominates the entire scientific scene" (Kantor, 1958, p.158).

In our view, the utility agenda does tend to dominate the work conducted in the applied subsystem, so much so that the applied subsystem can seem to be separate from the rest of the entire discipline of which it was originally a part. We see evidence of this when the applied subsystem constructs its own special philosophy of science concerned, for example, with notions of utility and truth. The former, utility, speaks to the pragmatic agenda directly. The latter, truth, violates one of the most fundamental assumptions of the philosophy of science from an interbehavioral perspective, namely freedom from absolutes. Readers interested in this topic are encouraged to read literature that has addressed these issues in more detail (e.g., Hayes, 1993; Hayes & Fryling, 2019).

The Interpretive Subsystem

Among the principal subsystems of behavior science is the interpretive subsystem. Kantor (1958) sees the interpretation of events as the primary goal of science. In his words, "Only when valid interpretive propositions can be formulated has the requisite understanding of events been achieved, an understanding which is basic to control and prediction" (Kantor, 1958, p.129). Interpretive subsystems consist of propositions abstracted from comprehensive scientific systems that serve to summarize and formalize the interrelations and significance of observed events.

Summary and Key Points

This chapter provided an overview of systems from an interbehavioral perspective. We specifically described system building as a process by which scientific systems are constructed and evaluated. We also described Kantor's pyramid of science, which depicts how cultural folklore, philosophy of science, scientific metasystems, and specific disciplinary assumptions participate in scientific systems. Examples of three specific tasks of system builders were described, as well as how individual scientific disciplines are conceptualized as systems within interbehavioral psychology. The conceptualization of sciences as systems, including the various subsystems, was described, as well as the implications of these analyses for continuing system development. The systems perspective is fundamental to the interbehavioral position, and there are many potential benefits of system building for both psychological science and the larger family of sciences.

Study Questions

1. What are the two ways the word "system" is used in the chapter?
2. Distinguish between validity and significance as they pertain to system building.
3. How does comprehensiveness participate in system building work?
4. Describe the cultural matrix in your own words.
5. Explain two of the metasystem assumptions in your own words. Why do you think these assumptions are particularly important?
6. What are the three tasks of the system builder as reviewed in the present chapter?
7. What is the applied subsystem? Explain the factors and concerns associated with the applied subsystem.

CHAPTER 3

Interbehavioral Psychology

The previous chapters have focused on the foundations of interbehaviorism as a philosophy of science (chapter 1) and have provided a description of the practice of system building, including the conceptualization of sciences as systems (chapter 2). In the present chapter we shift our attention to interbehavioral psychology. We begin with an overview of the assumptions pertinent to the science of psychology, focusing on its most fundamental construct, namely the interbehavioral field. The field construction is identified in part by contrasting it with causal constructions more typically employed in behavioral psychology. Following this is a more detailed description of the field construction itself, including explanations of the various factors participating in it.

Postulates of Interbehavioral Psychology

We begin with an outline of the assumptions of interbehavioral psychology, as described by

Kantor (1958, pp.77–82; Kantor & Smith, 1975, pp.415–17). These assumptions are at the top of the pyramid described in the previous chapter, and are thereby focused on the discipline specifically.

Postulate 1: Essential datum: Psychological events consist of multifactor fields.

The first postulate of interbehavioral psychology pertains to the construction of the subject matter itself. Psychological events are conceptualized as multifactor fields. Kantor (1958, p.77) claims that psychological events are in no way dualistic; they do not involve "manifestations of occult powers or forces," but instead involve concrete happenings. Moreover, as multifactor fields involve a range of factors, Kantor reminds us that "when in any given instance we are unable to observe the details of the interbehavior, we can only assume, as in all the other sciences, that this incapacity arises from nothing else than the intricacy of the events or the ineffectiveness of our techniques" (p.77). That is, being unaware of the details of a particular psychological event underscores its multifactored nature, as well as our inability to technically or conceptually capture all of the factors participating in it. Importantly, these limitations to our knowledge of the factors participating in a psychological event do not suggest that there is a hidden world or dimension, as is assumed from a dualistic perspective. This assumption is elaborated upon at length in the present chapter.

Postulate 2: Event interrelation: Psychological events are interrelated with social as well as with biological and physical events.

This postulate calls attention to the fact that psychological events, as events derived from the full matrix of natural happenings, are closely related to the events investigated in other sciences. The relation between the events of the psychological and biological domains is particularly close, which has been improperly exploited for explanatory purposes in other psychological perspectives. Further, as psychological events are conceptualized as relations between the responding of organisms and the stimulating of environing things, the physical and chemical properties of environing things are also relevant to an understanding of psychological events. To these we must add factors of a social and societal sort. As Kantor and Smith (1975, p.416) point out, "Psychologists cannot neglect the cultural properties of things." The cultural aspects of the subject matter are described in detail in part 2 of the text.

Postulate 3: Ecological evolution: Psychological events are evolved from ecological interbehavior.

Psychological events build upon biological interbehavior, interbehavior that is common to all members of a particular species. These include the basic reflexes that do not develop over the course of an individual's lifetime but rather over the course of species evolution. These ecological interbehaviors are the foundation upon which psychological behavior develops. This postulate calls attention to the fact that psychological events are elaborations upon ecological foundations. Over the course of an individual's lifetime, basic ecological interactions become more elaborated, and as they do, they become psychological in nature. Note that this realization that psychological events develop upon ecological foundations does not imply that psychological events are reducible to or otherwise caused by events of the ecological type.

Postulate 4: Whole organism action: Psychological events involve the

participation of total organisms, not merely special organs or tissues.

Interbehavioral psychology recognizes that psychological events involve the whole organism, the implication being that no part of the organism is more or less important than any other part. In Kantor's words, "Interbehavioral psychology does not attribute greater importance to any one structure than to any other, whether it be a cerebral or glandular organ or system" (1958, p.79). One implication of this postulate is that the distinction between public and private events, as proposed by Skinner (e.g., 1953, 1957) and others, is precluded. There are no events of the psychological type occurring on the parts of isolated internal organs from an interbehavioral perspective (see Hayes & Fryling, 2018 for further discussion). Psychological events are concrete happenings involving the participation of the whole organism.

Kantor (1977, p.127) further reflects on the theme of the whole organism postulate as follows: "We never make only one kind of contact with a stimulating object. We do not hear through our ears alone, but through our eyes, also. And conversely, we see things through our ears and touch reactions too. In all cases we do nothing less than act as a complete and complex person with all the numerous reaction systems which make a complex response to a stimulus situation, and which moreover may be influenced by a very elaborate setting." This quotation exemplifies the concept of whole organism action in interbehavioral psychology.

Postulate 5: Psychological events are ontogenic.

Psychological events are not species specific, as was the case for the aforementioned ecological interbehaviors. Rather, they develop and evolve over the course of an individual's lifetime. Psychological events are historical. This is to say, an individual's history of responding with respect to stimulation—their psychological history—is a participating factor in subsequent psychological happenings (more on this below).

Postulate 6: Variational details: Psychological interbehavior varies in specific details from other types of interbehavior.

While psychological events are interrelated with other sorts of events, psychological events are unique. As just discussed, psychological events are ontogenic, continuously changing over the course of an individual's lifetime. The same cannot be said of biological events. Biological events are relatively specific and constant (Kantor,

1958, p.80). Moreover, while the biological events of the neurological sort may be said to participate in psychological events, such events are not confused with psychological events per se. This postulate calls attention to the uniqueness of psychological events.

Postulate 7: Event construct continuity: Psychological constructions are continuous with crude data events.

Given that interbehavioral psychology is a natural science, the constructs developed and employed in this science are derived from contacts with events rather than from dualistic, religious, or other varieties of cultural folklore. In Kantor's (1958, p.81) words, "(T)he fact that scientists construct abstractions, descriptions, and laws concerning events is not to be confused with the belief that the events themselves are constructs." The point Kantor is making here is that observed events and descriptive constructions concerning them are different. Observation and description are different operations. This, in turn, means that it is possible to conceptualize events from different perspectives, specifically from the perspective of the events themselves and from that of the observer (see Parrott, 1986a).

Postulate 8: Causal principles: Psychological events consist of interrelated factors that do not admit internal or external determiners.

This postulate relates to the multifactor nature of psychological events. Psychological events are multifactored, with the participation of any one factor being no more important than any other. This proposition eliminates all notions of internal determiners of psychological events, including instincts, capacities, psyches, willpowers, and more. Also eliminated are external determiners, such as eliciting and reinforcing stimuli. "The alternative to the causal construction is the interbehavioral field" (Kantor, 1958, p.82).

These postulates of interbehavioral psychology are listed and translated into lay terms in table 3.1 (Kantor, 1958, pp.77–82; Kantor & Smith, 1975, pp.415–17).

Table 3.1. Sample Philosophical Postulates Pertaining to Interbehavioral Psychology

Original Language	Translation
Psychological events consist of multifactor fields.	The subject matter of the science of psychology is an interbehavioral field.
Psychological events are interrelated with social as well as biological and physical events.	Psychological events are closely related to sociological, biological, and physical events.

Psychological events are evolved from ecological interbehavior.	Psychological events develop from species-specific bioecological interbehavior (e.g., reflexes).
Psychological events involve the participation of total organisms, not merely special organs or tissues.	Psychological events are actions of the whole organism, not its parts considered separately.
Psychological events are ontogenetic.	Psychological events develop during the lifetime of the individual.
Psychological interbehavior varies in specific details from other types of interbehavior.	Psychological events are unique, different than other sorts of interactions.
Psychological constructions are continuous with crude-data events.	Psychological terms, theories, and more are derived from contacts with events.
Psychological events consist of interrelated factors that do not admit internal or external determiners.	Psychological events are not caused by anything internal or external. They consist of relationships among the factors participating in integrated fields.

As we have now considered the postulates of the science of interbehavioral psychology, we now turn to the construct of the interbehavioral field construct specifically. We begin with a consideration of the conceptual foundations of the interbehavioral field, and then consider the interbehavioral field itself in some detail.

Conceptual Foundations for the Field Construct

As we have emphasized in both chapter 1 and 2, Kantor's work, including both interbehaviorism and interbehavioral psychology, has a distinct natural science mission. At the most fundamental level, Kantor's (1953, 1958) aim was to eliminate all reference to hypothetical mental events as explanations of behavior. Kantor's aim in this regard was not unlike that of Skinner (1953, 1974), who also contributed to the development of a natural science of psychology. Both viewed the employment of hypothetical constructs for this purpose as a detriment to the progress of psychological science. Despite their agreement on aims, Kantor and Skinner approached progress toward the development of a natural science of psychology in different ways. Kantor's approach emphasized system building (chapter 2), whereas Skinner's approach was focused on investigation. When the means of pursuing a natural science are different, the sciences thus produced are different. For example, the practice of system building gives rise to the field construction of Kantor's interbehavioral psychology, while the practice of investigation gives rise to the causal construction of Skinner's behavior analytic psychology. Because this is the case, and these are especially significant issues, we elaborate on them a bit more in what follows before proceeding to the details of the interbehavioral field construct itself.

The emphasis on investigation as the primary means to develop a natural science of psychology is widespread in behavior analysis. In fact, so widespread is the assumption that research is the path to developing a natural science of behavior that some within mainstream behavior analysis appear to believe that science is investigation, investigation is science. In other words, there is some loosely held notion that science and investigation are synonymous. Further, the sort of research deemed to be science in this sense is a type of experimentation in which some factors are manipulated so as to reveal their causal relations with other factors. The emphasis on investigation in behavior analytic psychology has fostered the development of a natural science of behavior by permitting the measurement of observable behavior to changing environing factors to replace the imposition of explanatory hypothetical constructs. Given our natural science, this is a good thing. Nonetheless, continued coherent development of the science of psychology is not assured in the absence—even deliberate dismissal—of system building activity (chapter 2).

This emphasis on research in behavior analytic psychology stands in contrast to the perspective we are describing in this book. While research is needed to develop a natural science of psychology from an interbehavioral perspective, investigation is not synonymous with science. It is, rather, a subsystem of the science of behavior along with those of application and interpretation, as previously discussed in the last chapter.

Added to this, as Kantor noted (1958, p.3), the subject matter of behavior science is readily observable and available in great quantity. In this sense, there is little room for the discovery of new events in behavior science relative to the circumstances of many other scientific disciplines. Most events of the psychological type are already well known. Given this, it might be assumed that we would have acquired a highly sophisticated understanding of this subject matter by now. As most readers know well, this is not the case. What is needed for this purpose, according to Kantor, is a reconsideration of our fundamental constructions, including the definition of our subject matter and our premises concerning it. This chapter exemplifies the value of such a reconsideration. First, we provide a more detailed analysis of the foundations of behavior analytic psychology, including the definition of its subject matter and its incorporation of causal constructions.

Behavior analysts focus on relationships between stimulation and responding in their analyses of behavior. These relationships are of interest to interbehavioral psychologists as well, though their conceptualization of them differs in important ways. Specifically, behavior analysts tend to focus on dependency relations, whereby behavior (i.e., the dependent variable) is held to be dependent on various factors in the environment, be they things that occur before (e.g., discriminative stimuli) or after behavior (e.g., stimulus changes that are held to strengthen or select behavior) (see Skinner, 1974). The point is that behavior is held to be dependent on these factors: there is a cause (i.e., something in the environment) and an effect (i.e., behavior). This model is sometimes elaborated upon to explain complex behavior—for example, sometimes "causes of causes" are recognized, whereby the cause of an effect on behavior is caused by another factor. This happens in behavior analysis when the traditional three-term **contingency** is expanded to be four or five terms. The more expansive the analysis, the more causes of causes of causes that are needed. For example, a conditional stimulus is held to cause the discriminative stimulus to have its discriminative functions, which is then held to occasion behavior, a relation that exists because of a history of reinforcement, all of which ultimately causes behavior to occur.

In our experience, some behavior analysts disagree with our suggestion that causal relations are implied throughout the system. For the most part, it is argued that behavior analysts are not interested in causal relations, but rather functional relations, that is, R = f (S). While substituting the word "function" for "cause" is a step in the right direction, the problem remains in that "functional" relations continue to be interpreted as causal relations (see Fryling & Hayes, 2011, and Parrott, 1983a, for further discussion).

One last thing before moving on to the interbehavioral field construction warrants comment. Recall that behavior analysts, in emphasizing research as the path to developing a natural science of behavior, have taken research to be synonymous with science. One outcome of this is that dependency constructions appropriate in the context of the investigative subsystem are deemed appropriate in other subsystems, as well as in the philosophical foundations of the system more broadly. That is, we might confuse our methods of conducting and talking about manipulative research on behavior-stimulus relations with the behavior-stimulus relations themselves. Put differently, our subject matter should not be confused with how we talk about the manipulation of its parts in the context of investigation. This is a classic example of confusing constructs with events, as discussed in previous chapters.

Confusing constructs and events in psychology is due, in part, to its subject matter. For example, the subject matter of psychology, while ubiquitous, isn't a concrete thing, but rather a functional relationship between stimulation and responding. While relationships are genuine events and a valid subject matter, the lack of "thingness" may make the confusion between constructs and events more likely. Similarly, the functional relationships we are most interested in are not localized in the individual organism, but rather are participants in a complex field of many other factors. Behavior is also a continuously evolving stream of activity and may become more and more elaborate over time. Our subject matter also involves the behavior of the whole organism, and not its parts in isolation. In addition, we aren't interested in the relationship between stimulus objects and the responding organism, but in stimulus and response *functions*. This means that individuals may engage in implicit responding with respect to **substitute stimulus** functions (e.g., think about a friend when they hear a song). Readers interested in learning more about the unique features of psychological events, and how they pertain to the confusion of constructs with events, are encouraged to consult Fryling and Hayes (2009).

What is needed is an alternative formulation of the subject matter altogether. We now turn to the interbehavioral field.

The Interbehavioral Field

The interbehavioral field is how interbehavioral psychologists conceptualize the subject matter of their discipline. It is a distinct alternative to more traditional constructs in behavior analysis. While there is an interest in the relationship between stimulation and responding from an interbehavioral perspective, the relationship is conceptualized as a unitary happening, an interaction, whereby there is an interdependence of stimulation and responding. This conceptualization is illustrated by the use of a double-headed arrow between sf (stimulus function) and rf (response function), such that sf ↔ rf. Note that responding is not held to be an effect of a causal stimulus in this conceptualization. This is the reason why interbehaviorists prefer the word "interbehavior" as opposed to the more common term "behavior," to emphasize that behavior is not something that exists alone, a mere effect of something that happened before or after it. Rather, behavior is interbehavior, a unitary interaction among stimulation and responding, neither of which happens before or after the other.

As such, stimulation and responding are not considered to be separate things. They are one thing, one function. Interbehaviorists use the word "function" in a different way than most are accustomed to within behavior analysis. "Function" is used in a manner similar to how it is used in mathematics to describe a line as a unitary relationship (Kantor, 1950). The interrelation of stimulating and responding is the focal point of a psychological event, which we describe in more detail in the next section.

The Psychological Event

Interbehavioral psychologists conceptualize the interbehavioral field or psychological event with the following formula (Kantor, 1958, p.14):

PE = C (k, sf, rf, st, md, hi)

In this formula:

PE = The Psychological Event—This is another way of referring to the interbehavioral field or the "behavior segment." The terms are used somewhat synonymously. This is a unit event of the subject matter of the science of psychology from an interbehavioral perspective.

C = Indicates that the entire field of factors is one integrated whole.

k = Specifies that no one psychological event can be the identical to another event—as each is composed of a unique set and organization of factors.

sf and **rf** = Stimulus function and response function. Important in this regard is that stimulus functions are distinguished from stimulus objects, and response functions are distinguished from responding organisms.

st = Setting factors that are the immediate circumstances in the presence of which particular sf↔rf functions are taking place. Different sf↔rf functions occur in different settings.

md = Media of contact refers to the means through which a biological organism contacts a physical stimulus object.

hi = The **interbehavioral history** that represents the reactional biography and the evolution of stimulus functions (sf↔rf functions) throughout the organism's history.

A number of issues and implications posed by this description of the psychological event warrant further clarification and elaboration. The first of these pertains to the factor **C** in the formula. This factor symbolizes the notion that the psychological event is an integrated whole. The implication of this is that the addition, removal, or manipulation of any factor in the situation changes the entire event, such that it may be considered a different event. Importantly, this means that changing one thing doesn't "cause a change" in another thing, because everything is one integrated happening. The understanding that each and every psychological event is a unique event is indicated by the factor **k** in the formula.

·

Stimulus and Response Function. The psychological event also calls attention to both stimulus function and response function. The inclusion of the word "function" here is to draw attention to the distinction between stimuli as functions (or actions) from stimuli as objects or sources of functions, and responses as functions (or actions) from organisms as sources of responses. This distinction has several implications for the understanding of complex behavior, which are addressed in more detail in part 2 of this book. For present purposes, the topic of memory may serve to highlight the value of this distinction. Despite the fact that people frequently reminisce about their past experiences, behavior analytic psychology has offered very little understanding of this type of activity. For example, Skinner noted that in such cases people are responding to stimuli in their absence (1974, pp.82–83). Holding to the premise that there is no stimulating without responding, no responding without stimulating—as we do—Skinner's idea on this matter is of no help. The question to be answered in this regard is, what are we interacting with when we think about the past? From an interbehavioral perspective, there is surely something in the present circumstance that has acquired the function of the past experience. When a present stimulus has the functional properties of an absent stimulus, we say that the present stimulus is substituting for the absent stimulus. For example, a picture of a friend may harbor substitute stimulus functions of experiences established with that friend at a previous time. In this case, the picture is a stimulus object through which substitute stimulus functions are operating. Similarly, response functions, or **implicit behavior,** involves responding with respect to substitute stimulation. Implicit responding cannot occur without substitute stimulation and substitute stimulation cannot occur without implicit responding. This again emphasizes that stimulating and responding constitute a unitary phenomenon.

Kantor (1924, 1926) and other interbehaviorists propose that substitute stimulation develops under conditions of association. Association conditions are circumstances where an individual responds with respect to stimulation in a context in which two or more factors are occurring together in space-time. Association conditions can occur among stimuli and responses, stimuli and stimuli, settings and stimuli, settings and settings, and so on (e.g., Kantor, 1924, p.321). Conditions of association are always present and as long as an individual responds with respect to the factors involved in those conditions, substitute stimulus functions may develop. Given such a history of responding with respect to factors under various conditions of association, at a later time when only one of the factors is present, responding with respect to the absent factor may occur. For example, a history of hearing a friend's voice while also seeing their face may result in seeing their face while hearing the friend's voice on the telephone (i.e., in the absence of the visual stimulus of the face). In this sense, the sound of the friend's voice is substituting for the visual stimulation of their face. There are countless examples of how these processes may be involved in cases of complex behavior, all without speculating about responding in the absence of stimulus objects, internal happenings, or memory storage bins. This topic is closely related to interbehavioral history, to which we now turn.

.

Interbehavioral History. Interbehavioral history, represented by **hi** in the formula for the psychological event, involves the evolution and elaboration of stimulus-response functions over an individual's history. In other words, an individual's sf↔rf history is present in the stimulus functions of the current psychological event. The past, in this sense, is present in the setting (Hayes, 1992b). The implication of this is that while psychological events are continuously evolving, and therefore historical in nature, interbehavioral history is not held to be responsible for the actualization of particular functions in a given psychological event field. This stands in contrast to more mechanistic forms of behaviorism, where the past is assumed to determine the present. From an interbehavioral perspective, the sf↔rf functions obtaining in particular event fields at particular points in time simply reflect their evolution up to that point.

.

Setting Factors. The setting, represented by **st** in the formula for a psychological event, is a situation, composed of many factors, in the presence of which some particular sf↔rf relation is momentarily taking place. The sf↔rf relation is the focus of the psychological event from an observer's perspective (Parrott, 1983c). Setting factors are not limited to features of the environment. They also include conditions of the responding individual, such as illness, fatigue, intoxication, and so on. Any given setting is made up of an enormous number of factors. Among them are objects that have been sources of stimulus functions at previous times. Some of these functions may arise directly from their object properties, while others are substitutive. Setting factors, while not the focus of a present psychological event as stated above, are nonetheless relevant to that event in the sense that were they to be different, a different sf↔rf relation would be actualized. This is all to say that setting factors are part of the present event. They are participating factors.

.

Medium of Contact. Kantor's description of the psychological event also includes the medium of contact **(md).** The medium of contact generally refers to factors that permit psychological events to occur. For example, visual perceptual events involve light, hearing events involve sound waves, and so on. These factors pertain more to direct interactions with stimuli, and less to more indirect or substitutive stimulus functions. For instance, imagining someone's face while hearing their voice does not involve the light that would be required for a direct, non-implicit seeing response with respect to their face. As this example highlights, it is important to avoid confusing the medium of contact with the stimulus itself. Media of contact are not stimulus factors.

Summary and Key Points

This chapter focused on interbehavioral psychology, including the postulates that serve to organize the work in this field of study. The chapter then considered the interbehavioral field construct, the psychological event, as described in interbehavioral psychology. The interbehavioral field is a descriptive construction that represents a unit of the subject matter of interbehavioral psychology. As the interbehavioral field is construed as a single, unified happening, all notions of one part of the event (a response) being caused by another part of the event (a stimulus) are ruled out of consideration. This stands in contrast to more traditional ways of conceptualizing the subject matter from a behavioral perspective, especially those involving contingency constructs wherein some factors are deemed to be more important or causal than others (e.g., reinforcers).

This chapter is an introductory overview of the assumptions of interbehavioral psychology and the field construction. Kantor's conceptualization of stimulus substitution and implicit responding are particularly relevant to the analysis of complex behavior, which is the focus of part 2 of the book. Similarly, the participation of setting factors as sources of interbehavioral history have far-reaching implications for research and practice. We elaborate upon these topics in the following two chapters.

Study Questions

1. In your own words, describe the postulate that states, "Psychological events consist of multifactor fields."

2. How does postulate 8, "Causal principles: Psychological events consist of interrelated factors which do not admit internal or external determiners," relate to the postulate in question 1?

3. Describe two other postulates of interbehavioral psychology, including their implications for behavior analysis and psychology more generally.

4. Compare and contrast Kantor's and Skinner's aims, particularly as described in the

section "Conceptual Foundations for the Field Construct."

5. Why is the confusion between constructs and events especially likely in psychology?

6. What is the significance of the letter *C* in the psychological event formula?

7. What are association conditions and how do they pertain to the development of substitute stimulus functions and implicit responding?

CHAPTER 4

Interbehavioral Research

Chapter 3 provided an overview of interbehavioral psychology. The present chapter builds upon chapter 3 by describing the implications of the interbehavioral field construct for research. While it is important to remember that a psychological event is conceptualized as an integrated field from an interbehavioral perspective, in this chapter, for analytical purposes, we will focus on two aspects of the field construct somewhat independently. In particular, we will focus on the interbehavioral history and the setting. We begin with a brief review of some pertinent philosophical assumptions (from chapter 1) and then move on to some examples of areas where the field construct may be especially useful for behavior analytic researchers.

Philosophical Assumptions Pertinent to Research

Recall that the previous chapter described how research is a topic that reflects some of the core differences between interbehavioral and more traditional behavioral approaches, especially as pertains to the means of developing a science of psychology. For example, Skinner (1938) placed heavy emphasis on experimental research as a means of developing a natural science of psychology—so much so, in fact, that research is sometimes confused with science as a whole. By contrast, Kantor (1953) emphasized the utility of system building for this purpose (chapter 2). This is not to suggest that research is unimportant or insignificant in interbehavioral psychology. Quite the opposite, actually. In Kantor's (1953) words, "To emphasize experimentation in science is to pay a signal tribute to our constantly stressed interbehavioral principle that science proceeds on the basis of contacts with things and events" (p.101). Interbehaviorism proposes that all constructs be derived from contacts with events, and research involves especially close contact with the events of interest. Research is an essential feature of a scientific system.

With that being said, there are some foundational assumptions that require further consideration before we address the implications of the interbehavioral field construction for research. First, from an interbehavioral perspective, research is not a means of *demonstrating* or *proving* something to be *real* or *true*. Recall from chapter 1 that interbehaviorism rejects all notions of absolute reality and universal truth. These are neither the aims nor the outcomes of research. Rather, research is a descriptive, discovery-oriented endeavor. It is aimed at describing the relationships among the factors participating in interbehavioral fields. Note that the word "descriptive" in this context is not delimiting (as when someone says "that's merely descriptive"), but rather acknowledges that *all research is descriptive in nature*.

When scientists assume that research is more than this—when research is taken to be the arbiter of truth about reality—missteps are likely to occur. Kantor (1953) suggests that science is viewed as "magic" when scientists assume that "a set of operations (demonstrations) would definitely and permanently settle scientific questions" (p.109). When science is understood in this way, researchers tend to feel the need to demonstrate everything, in every which way, so as to *prove* their findings to be true. We notice this when study after study is pursued with the aim of *demonstrating* that some set of operations works the same way in some slightly different context or with ever so slightly different parameters. For example, treatment X may be studied in dozens of different situations, under the "demonstrate and prove" principle, yet still be seen as needing further study in another context where it hasn't so far been *proven* to be effective. In short, research, as mere manipulation, can become rather dull and routine when notions of reality and truth aren't specifically rejected.

The alternative to this sort of magical thinking is to recognize that science is cumulative and corrigible. There is no truth about reality to demonstrate in ever more ingenious sets of operations. Research is an enterprise aimed at the discovery and description of correlations among factors participating in an integrated field. This isn't to say that replication, that repeating an investigation, is not important. However, replications themselves may be pursued and interpreted differently when notions of reality and truth are eliminated from the research agenda. All of this is to say that assumptions about the aims of research impact what research questions are asked, how the results are interpreted, and more. This is the overarching theme of the present chapter.

While there's no place for reality and truth in interbehavioral psychology, questions concerning the utility of methods and value of their results are another matter. Importantly, though, the utility agenda is derived from applied interests, and should be recognized and appreciated as such. In other words, research questions related to the utility or value of some treatment or intervention are derived from the applied subsystem of a scientific discipline (see chapter 2) and are applicable to matters with which that particular domain is concerned (see Fryling, 2011, 2013b; Hayes & Fryling, 2019). Put differently, the notion that utility *per se* is the value toward which all scientific work is aimed is to overvalue the applied domain at the expense of the other subsystems of the scientific enterprise, in addition to its foundational philosophy (also Hayes et al., 2009).

When the foundational assumptions regarding the aims of research are understood and embraced—namely, avoiding notions of reality and truth, and embracing a discovery orientation for scientific research—we might begin to explore other things. And we might wonder just exactly *what* other interests we might pursue. In short, if we have all been trained to pursue research with the more or less explicitly held aims of achieving truth about reality, where do we go from here? This is where the interbehavioral field construct (chapter 3) can be of service. The field construct calls attention to various factors present in psychological events, and specifically emphasizes how each factor participates in the integrated whole. That is, there is no emphasis placed on one factor being more or less important or influential relative to the others. In other words, there are a *lot* of things that could be studied. The following sections focus on two such things, interbehavioral history and setting conditions. Following this, we will comment on the subdomain of interpretation in interbehavioral psychology.

Interbehavioral History

Both scientists and laypersons alike acknowledge that what happened in a person's past behavior influences (or is, at least, important to) their present behavior. Despite this widespread understanding, relatively little behavioral research has focused on interbehavioral history. There may be several reasons for this neglect. Among them are the fact that the details of a person's history are largely unknown and otherwise hard to control for or measure, a view that assumes the history to be absent from the present circumstance. In most conceptualizations of behavior, *the past is the past.* As outlined in the previous chapter, though, interbehavioral history refers to the many ways an individual's history with respect to the focal sf↔rf interaction is present in the interbehavioral field. In other words, from an interbehavioral perspective, *the past is the present* (Hayes, 1992b). Specifically, the past is present in the functions of stimuli comprising the setting. This perspective on the past depends on a distinction between stimuli as objects and stimuli as functions, a distinction that has not been fully appreciated in more traditional approaches to behavioral psychology. Importantly, not only is the past the present in interbehavioral psychology, but it is also a participating factor in the integrated field. As such, it is available for and worthy of investigation.

Recognizing that history is crucial to the understanding of psychological happenings, researchers may begin to study it. In general, we might ask, "How do various histories participate in psychological events?" History participates in all psychological events and has implications for various areas of research. We describe some of these areas below. In doing so we do not claim specific expertise in these areas, but rather highlight how the interbehavioral history might be explored.

Psychotherapy Research. The realm of psychotherapy research presents many opportunities for exploring interbehavioral history. Researchers could explore how a client's history with different therapies, therapists, or life experiences participate in the way in which a particular intervention is functionally (i.e., descriptively) related to therapy targets (i.e., a behavior change). Similarly, the histories of therapists may be explored, including the extent to which a therapist has worked with a particular population, used different techniques, been exposed to different types of training, and so on. Any of these issues could be studied in an analog manner prior to their observation in a therapeutic context. For example, particular histories could be developed prior to exposure to an intervention in an analog setting involving relatively arbitrary stimuli. The number of factors of this type that could be explored are countless. More importantly, a study of these factors would be of great service in efforts to understand behavior in a therapeutic context. Unfortunately, current research practices may encourage researchers to control for these factors, or to view them as confounds that inhibit demonstration-based research agendas.

.

ABA-Based Instruction. A similar case for the study of history may be made in more traditional applied behavior analytic research on instructional practices. It is well known that particular instructional histories are likely to be participating in current instructional efforts and their participation is, thereby, likely to be related to learning outcomes. Despite recognition of this circumstance, relatively little study of interbehavioral histories with respect to applied behavior analytic research has been reported. For example, one factor that may be relevant to the outcomes of behavioral research on instructional practices is the length of participants' previous exposure to interventions based on the principles and practices of applied behavior analysis (e.g., differential reinforcement, prompting, etc.). Surprisingly little is known about how interbehavioral histories participate in instructional outcomes in ABA instructional research. Similar to our previous example, it seems that it is more often the case that instructional histories would be best ignored or controlled for, so as to rule them out as potential confounds in demonstration-based research agendas.

A long line of research conducted by Greer and colleagues has pertained to the general question of the participation of interbehavioral history (e.g., Greer et al., 2020; Greer & Ross, 2008; Greer & Speckman, 2009). Much of this line of research has focused on the development of verbal behavior in particular, and it is noteworthy for specifically aiming to understand which instructional experiences lead to the development of more complex skills (i.e., what needs to happen before another instructional experience will be successful). Delineating the details of this lengthy research program is far beyond the scope of the present chapter, but it is mentioned here as an example of how research sensitive to interbehavioral history might be pursued. Specifically, this type of research provides a behavioral-developmental guide that indicates *when* a particular instructional intervention is more or less likely to be successful, and further, what to do when an intervention is not successful. Bringing things back to our interest in history, the larger research program draws attention to how different histories participate in present psychological events.

•

Therapist-Client Relationship Histories. Similarly, we know very little about how different histories of therapists working with participants in research studies impact results of investigation. For example, a therapist who has worked with a client for many weeks or months prior to a study may have a different outcome than a therapist who has little or no history working with this person. In other words, we might find out what sorts of therapist-client histories lead to the most beneficial results. Not only would this line of research be informative, but it would also have implications for how therapists are trained and supervised. Similar to other areas, it would be easy to formulate analog models of therapist-client histories, whereby more basic functional relations may be discovered.

•

Consultee Training Research. Interbehavioral history also seems likely to play a role in the success of various parent, caregiver, and/or teacher training interventions. Oftentimes consultees have already experienced a lengthy history of attempting to change a client's behavior. This may have involved implementing various strategies on a trial-and-error basis, following the recommendations of another therapist, the individual's teacher, extended family members, and more. By the time the consultee is interacting with the current behavior therapist, they aren't just interacting with the current therapist, but also with historical recommendations from various sources that are participating in the present circumstance. Again, we know little about how to tailor our work with consultees who have varying histories of attempting to change client behavior. At the same time, this is exactly the sort of research that would be valuable to consultants in their work with consultees.

While these are just examples of how the concept of an interbehavioral history may encourage us to ask discovery-oriented research questions, they also highlight an important point based in interbehavioral thinking. Too often, especially in applied research programs, research is pursued with the assumption that the study will either prove that the intervention *works* or *doesn't work*, and nothing more than that. Overlooked in all of this is the fact that interventions are *not things that exist separately from the context in which they are studied.* Interventions are *manipulations*—additions to a complex interbehavioral field. As such, they *participate in that field*, along with everything else. When interventions work or don't work, they do so as participants in an integrated field of many other factors. Given this, intervention outcomes tell us only a very small part of the story.

Basic Research. Interbehavioral history may be a source of valuable information in the context of basic research as well, and such research is the principal means by which our understanding of functional relations becomes more precise. It also serves as a means by which theories are refined, methods are improved, and designs better adapted to particular types of events. We have noticed some examples of interbehavioral history being explored in basic research conceptualized in terms of relational frame theory (Hayes et al., 2001) in recent years. For example, research by Barnes-Holmes and colleagues (2020b) has examined how different histories with stimuli impact participants' responses on the implicit relational assessment procedure (IRAP). These findings came about while the authors were conducting research involving stimuli that are frequently contacted in the natural environment (i.e., colors). In particular, when these more frequently contacted stimuli are included in IRAP arrangements, distinct patterns of responding have been found. In other words, individuals' histories with respect to stimuli were present in their current interactions (e.g., Finn et al., 2018).

This same research group has also conducted research on rule-governed behavior, examining how specific histories of rule-following are present in current psychological events (e.g., Harte et al., 2017). While we cannot speak to the nuances of this research here, including how it has been interpreted, it stands out as a line of work that is specifically studying interbehavioral history. It also seems that it represents a broader move toward a field-based view of derived relational responding (Barnes-Holmes et al., 2020a). We mention this line of research as an example of how basic behavioral research may begin to explore interbehavioral history as a feature of ongoing psychological happenings.

Our aim in this section was to highlight some areas where interbehavioral history might be incorporated into psychological research. Many of the examples we described focused on applied research, but there are opportunities for both basic and applied researchers to explore this important factor. Given the extent to which history is present in psychological happenings it seems incumbent upon us to explore it more seriously. The next section looks at another aspect of the interbehavioral field, namely setting conditions, and how they might be explored in psychological research.

Setting Conditions

As in the case of interbehavioral history, most researchers would assume that setting conditions, or situational factors, participate in ongoing psychological events in important ways.

Despite the recognition of the participation of setting conditions, relatively little is known about *how* setting conditions participate in psychological events. Indeed, if any information about the setting is provided in descriptions of psychological research, it is typically information that doesn't seem relevant to an understanding of any particular type of psychological happening. For example, in basic research studies, information may be provided about the dimensions of the room where the research is taking place, the type of software being used, and the size of the stimuli. In applied research, we are also told where research sessions were conducted (e.g., "at a table with two chairs"), what items were present on the table (e.g., datasheet, toys), and other types of procedural information. Again, little or no information is provided about setting conditions that may be specifically relevant to the phenomena under investigation.

Moreover, when setting conditions *are* studied in behavior analytic research, they often consist of a relatively narrow range of conditions. For example, inspired by the motivating operations concept (e.g., Michael, 1993; Laraway et al., 2003), behavior analysts have studied how subsequent behavior with respect to particular stimuli is impacted by prior restriction of access to them (e.g., restricting access to a preferred item and then measuring the extent to which this operation is associated with increases in requests for that item). While these sorts of studies are important and help identify factors that are functionally related to particular types of behavior change, they often pertain to a relatively narrow range of psychological happenings. In our view, this narrowness is related to problems with the motivating operations concept itself, especially its close relationship to the operant contingency, and linear, causal thinking more generally (see Hayes & Fryling, 2014 for a critique of the motivational operation concept).

The expansive role of setting conditions has yet to be fully explored in behavioral research. In the following examples we consider how setting conditions might be studied in various types of psychological research. We again consider potential examples from psychotherapy, ABA-based instruction, consultation, and basic research.

Psychotherapy Research. Therapists certainly recognize that situational factors influence the process and outcome of therapy in important ways. One setting factor that may be especially relevant pertains to the circumstances surrounding the initiation of therapy. For example, whether the individual starting therapy is doing so in a crisis state or as a means of meeting a social (e.g., a requirement from a significant other) or legal demand would seem to be important in this regard. Further, therapy is funded in different ways, and this may also be viewed as a setting condition. It seems likely that an individual paying for therapy out of pocket may have different expectations and exhibit different behaviors than one whose therapy sessions are being covered by insurance, for example. Similarly, it seems likely that the physical setting itself is related to how different interventions participate in psychological events (e.g., how the office or center is arranged). Finally, while many research studies are aimed at understanding the effects of some particular intervention on a particular category of symptoms (e.g., effects of treatment X on symptom A), symptom A doesn't exist independently of other symptoms and the conditions under which they present. In other words, how do other setting conditions, such as family dynamics, current relationship status, and career, interact such as to contribute to the presence of symptom A? These factors would be better explored than controlled for.

ABA-Based Instruction. Likewise, much of what we know about typical ABA-based instructional research is known without much information about setting factors. For example, the physical space in which interventions are implemented differs in various ways. Sometimes instruction is implemented in a clinic setting with very few clients and many staff present, perhaps even in a treatment room, whereas other times instruction is implemented at home with one therapist and family members present. Even when some of these factors are mentioned they are not explored in nearly enough detail. We might wonder whether an instructional intervention carried out in an environment that was quiet and free from distraction would have a different outcome than one carried out in a more naturalistic setting (i.e., one with uncontrolled noise, people coming and going, etc.). In the absence of a field perspective, these issues may seem less important or even trivial. However, viewing these issues in this way is an outcome of causal thinking (e.g., as when someone assumes "the contingencies are the contingencies"). Alternatively, when our subject matter is conceptualized from the perspective of an interbehavioral field there tends to be more curiosity about other, previously overlooked, factors.

In addition to the setting conditions that may be relevant to ABAbased interventions more generally, there are setting conditions unique to particular areas of application, such as childhood feeding problems. For example, the characteristics of the individuals participating in feeding research are likely to be an important factor. Consuming food involves various activities, including grasping utensils, chewing, and swallowing, among other things. Various developmental conditions may function as organismic setting factors that make any one of these steps more or less difficult or aversive. Thus, in addition to discovering which operations are most effective, researchers may have to consider which interventions are most effective and with which particular children, where additional setting factors are present. This conceptualization of the setting could no doubt be applied to many areas of research in ABA. Again, embracing an interbehavioral field-based approach may involve conducting research that takes us beyond demonstration-based investigation.

Consultee Training. Setting factors also participate in psychological events involved in research on effective consultee training strategies (e.g., many subsumed under behavioral skills training). This work has largely been conducted under the assumption that consultees lack knowledge and skills and, therefore, training is focused on teaching those skills directly by practices of modeling, rehearsal, feedback, and so on. Additional lines of research have focused on the topic of treatment integrity (the extent to which interventions are implemented as prescribed), where we have generally learned that improved integrity is associated with better clinical outcomes, and moreover, that certain types of integrity failures are more or less problematic (e.g., reinforcing the wrong behavior relative to omitting a prompt).

Relatively less is known about the circumstances under which consultees have been properly trained to implement interventions but do not continue to do so over time. In these circumstances it seems likely that setting factors need to be considered. For example, a parent may be exhausted, be experiencing marital or other relationship stressors, and/or lack a supportive and validating social network. The presence or absence of any of these factors is likely to influence implementation in important ways. As these examples suggest, it may be useful to conduct research on the setting conditions in this area (also see Fryling, 2014).

Basic Behavioral Research. There are substantial opportunities to explore setting conditions in basic, analog arrangements. If we were to think of the previous example of consultee implementation specifically, one could imagine developing a basic study where participants are taught to engage in a task in a particular way depending on the circumstances (e.g., to model the training part of the consultation described above). Then, after participants demonstrate their competency in this task (i.e., "implementation"), researchers could manipulate setting factors to determine their role in ongoing implementations. For example, participants could be required to engage in other tasks at the same time they are required to implement the intervention, so as to model the common consultee challenge of distracting circumstances. Similarly, participants could be required to engage in a difficult task for a relatively longer period of time before being asked to implement the intervention, to model challenges associated with implementing an intervention while considerably fatigued. Once a general model like this is established more nuanced manipulations of the setting could be conducted. As these examples show, the opportunities to explore setting conditions in more basic behavioral research are endless.

We have considered only a few ways in which the field orientation could contribute to research efforts in behavioral psychology. The interbehavioral field orientation also has implications for how we *interpret* research, and the interpretive subsystem is an important part of any scientific discipline (chapter 2). The following section focuses on this topic and is followed by a brief consideration of research methods from an interbehavioral perspective.

Interpretation

As we have now considered, the interbehavioral field construction has many implications for behavioral research enterprises, including how lines of research may be initiated and how the types of data relevant to the questions asked may be collected. These activities do not exhaust those entailed in a fully articulated scientific system. Also important are how we go about interpreting the outcomes of research. That is, asking research questions and gathering data is one thing; talking about the data and how it relates to the fundamental assumptions of the scientific system and its unique subject matter is quite another.

Here again we notice differences between more traditional and interbehavioral ways of thinking. From a more traditional perspective, where the purpose of research is to prove the value of something, interpretation is rightly limited to discerning the extent to which a hypothesis or theory has been proven to be correct or incorrect, with calls for additional ways of proving this to be the case in future research. For example, traditional practices of interpreting the outcomes of behavioral research are aimed at finding explanations for the outcomes achieved. Explanations, as sought in these contexts, are ways of referring to the causes of these outcomes, which tend to be discovered in the no longer present past or in other subject matters. Behaviorists of the Skinnerian tradition look for causes in both locations, neither of which turn out to be fruitful (Hayes et al., 1997). We have been discussing the problem with attempting to locate the causes of behavior in the no longer existing past (chapter 3). The deviation to another subject matter, namely in the biology of the behaving organism, is also a dead end on the grounds that what is happening in the organism is deemed inaccessible to the contemporary behavioral researcher (e.g., as when thinking is interpreted as a "private event"; more on this in chapter 7). Both of these strategies abandon the overarching aim of developing a thoroughgoing, natural science of behavior.

By contrast, from an interbehavioral perspective, interpretation is the means by which the investigative and applied subsystems of a science are held together by common definitions of the subject matter, adherence to common practices of primary and elaborate description, and overall adherence to the underlying philosophical foundations of that system. Interpretation in interbehavioral psychology is the practice of describing relations among previously described relations. It is not a search for causes.

A great deal of data has been collected by psychological researchers of different varieties over the years. Much of these data have been interpreted as being related to factors that cannot, in principle, be confronted, as opposed to factors of the confrontable environment. When research agendas are plagued by these sorts of philosophies, then the research questions asked, as well as the way in which the results are interpreted, are impacted. Subsequent research elaborates upon these assumptions, and entire fields of dualistic thinking develop.

By contrast, much of the work of interbehavioral psychologists is focused on articulating an *alternative* to these dualistic approaches. Still, the *data* collected by these nonbehavioral researchers may be of interest to us. That is, we might *reinterpret* existing research in ways aligned with our aims and constructs (e.g., from the perspective of the interbehavioral field). This would not only suggest that the interbehavioral approach is comprehensive and relevant, but also help build upon the interbehavioral system itself.

Research Methods

We conclude our chapter with a brief consideration of research methods from an interbehavioral perspective. It may seem a bit odd to have a chapter on the topic of research with so little attention to methods, but that points to more overarching themes in understanding the interbehavioral approach. That is, whereas methods may be seen as *the* way of demonstrating something, proving a causal relationship, in traditional ways of thinking, this is not the case for interbehavioral research. Indeed, if research becomes more descriptive in nature, then the exact *way* in which one goes about collecting data, manipulating the interbehavioral field, is less important. In fact, some methods which might otherwise be overlooked or dismissed could be of interest to interbehavioral researchers. For example, some interbehaviorists have noted their interest in Q-methodology (e.g., Brown, 2006) and other observational and qualitative methods (e.g., Verplanck, 1970). In Kantor's words, "It is a conventional view that experimentation does not begin until manipulation is reached. Observation, however, is not something entirely different from manipulation, nor manipulation from transformation" (1953, p.103). This quote lends itself to the idea that many research methods may be embraced in interbehavioral research.

Further, when one understands the interbehavioral field, including what it is not, terms associated with more traditional research practices might warrant reconsideration. For example, ideas of independent and dependent variables, holding some variables constant, ruling out confounds, returning to baseline conditions, and so on are difficult to sustain from an interbehavioral view. We agree with this, but at the same time remind readers that these terms are just ways of speaking that may be appropriate or even critical in the context of the investigative subsystem (chapter 2). The important thing to remember is that these ways of speaking ought not be confused with the rest of the scientific system. That is, when we interpret the results of some particular research and conceptualize subsequent studies, we need to remember that we are always looking to characterize the complex, multifactored interbehavioral field of which they are a part.

Summary and Key Points

This chapter provided an overview of the topic of research from an interbehavioral perspective. This included a consideration of philosophical assumptions related to understanding research, as well as examples of how interbehavioral history and setting factors might be explored in behavioral research. The chapter concluded by addressing the role of interpretation in research and a brief consideration of research methods.

Study Questions

1. It is sometimes thought that interbehaviorism doesn't value research. What does the chapter have to say about this?

2. How does the interbehavioral approach to research pertain to the rejection of absolute reality and ultimate truth, as described in chapter 1?

3. Under what circumstances might research become rather dull and routine?

4. Comment on the utility aim, including potential concerns when applied, when utility-based aims are confused with those of science more generally.

5. Explain what research is and is not from the perspective of the chapter.

6. How is the setting condition concept broader than the more common operant concept of motivating operations?

7. Describe the relationship between research and interpretation.

CHAPTER 5

Interbehavioral Application

This chapter focuses on the topic of application. We recognize that many of the readers of this text may be involved in applied practice in one way or another, as behavioral therapists, applied behavior analysts (e.g., BCBAs®), or perhaps as trainers and educators of the aforementioned professions. While there are a number of philosophical and systemic implications of interbehavioral work pertaining to the applied domain (see chapter 2 and also Fryling, 2011, 2013b), this chapter is about the implications of the interbehavioral field construct, including our elaborations and extensions of it, for applied work. This chapter will draw attention to some of the ways in which a field perspective may be helpful, and, in doing so, will contrast the field perspective with more common ways of conceptualizing applied issues, particularly those derived from the more traditional operant, contingency-based paradigm. We will consider the topics of functional behavioral assessment, behavioral consultation, and behavioral psychotherapy as examples. We begin with topics especially relevant to the practice area of applied behavior analysis, and focus on functional behavioral assessment and function-based interventions.

Assessment and Intervention

Behavioral assessment is distinguished from traditional psychological assessment in a number of ways. A core difference pertains to the fact that behavioral assessment doesn't aim to identify an inner personality trait or disorder, psychic conflict, or other internal entity that is then assumed to be responsible for an individual's behavior. Rather, behavioral assessment involves the measurement of behavior in some way, with an emphasis on understanding the factors that participate in the occurrence of that behavior (note our deliberate use of the word "participate" rather than "cause" or even "influence" here). As with many things in the behavioral tradition, the behavioral assessment model has long been influenced by the work of B.F. Skinner and others interested in his work, meaning there is a distinct operant, antecedent-behavior-consequence, approach to it. Much of this work has been related to what Skinner referred to as the functional analysis of behavior (e.g., Skinner, 1953, p.35). In fact, the functional analysis model aimed to identify the "causes of behavior" (p.35). We note this here because, while we prefer to talk about behavior in a particular interbehavioral way, the functional behavioral assessment model has a specific, linear foundation to it. We elaborate more on this below.

Functional Behavioral Assessment

Within the practice of ABA, "functional behavioral assessment" (FBA) is a broad term that refers to a general process aimed at understanding the operant contingencies that are assumed to be responsible for the maintenance of a target behavior. The model is known for involving three general assessment methods: indirect, descriptive, and experimental functional analysis (Fisher et al., 2021; Peterson & Neef, 2019). Indirect assessments involve interviews or checklists aimed at gathering information from informants about the behavior of interest and the contingencies that are assumed to maintain its occurrence. These interviews are helpful in that they serve to gather contextual information and inform hypotheses about potential maintaining variables. At the same time, it is important to remember that these assessments are based on informant perspectives, and point only to possible contingencies that maintain the behavior of interest. Moreover, some of these interview-based assessments are not designed to be rich sources of contextual information. Rather, they involve simple checklists that screen for predetermined factors assumed to be responsible for the occurrence of the target behavior, using formulas to come up with a score to identify the most influential contingency (see Fryling & Baires, 2016, for more on the strengths and weaknesses associated with these various instruments).

The second phase of the FBA process involves descriptive assessment. A descriptive assessment involves gathering information about operant contingencies from observations of the behavior as it occurs in the natural environment. For example, a clinician may observe a child in a classroom at a school, an employee at a job site, and more. Like indirect assessments, descriptive assessments may also involve forms with predetermined antecedents and consequences to check for, or alternatively be more open-ended. Importantly, this phase of the assessment is also conducted from the perspective of the operant contingency, and further, typically with the aim of identifying *particular* contingencies (e.g., attention, escape, tangible, or automatic reinforcement). This type of assessment is often held to be limited, because of the fact that it is merely descriptive in nature (e.g., Iwata et al., 2000, p.75). The idea is that descriptive assessments merely identify correlations that need to be confirmed with experimental manipulation.

Finally, the last step in the FBA model involves a functional analysis. A functional analysis can take many forms, but always involves the specific testing of possible contingencies identified in both the indirect and the descriptive assessments. For example, if there is a hypothesis that a target behavior is being maintained by negative reinforcement (e.g., the removal of instructions in a classroom), a functional analysis would involve specifically providing that consequence contingent on behavior, and not at other times, with the aim of evaluating its effect on behavior. The idea behind this is that if the behavior occurs more when this contingency is in place relative to when it is not, then this contingency is the maintaining variable (leaving room for the possibility that there may be multiple contingencies found to be maintaining the behavior). Moreover, the functional analysis is conceptualized as being superior to both the indirect and the descriptive assessments as it is seen as demonstrating functional relations (e.g., Iwata et al., 2000, p.71). The FBA model has been associated with a great deal of research in ABA, and there have been a range of variations in procedures that have been explored (e.g., Beavers et al., 2013; Fisher et al., 2021). Perhaps most importantly, the FBA model is noteworthy for turning the focus away from individuals as causes of their own behavior and toward understanding the context in which target behavior occurs.

Function-Based Intervention

As we have mentioned, the FBA model has had a tremendous influence on the practice of

ABA. Most noteworthy is the focus on interventions based on positive reinforcement derived from the use of the FBA model, and the reduction of aversive techniques. Indeed, the focus on identifying contingencies maintaining the behavior of interest has direct implications for the development of function-based intervention plans. We won't elaborate on intervention in much detail here, rather just consider a couple of examples. A behavior found to be maintained by social positive reinforcement may be treated with an intervention that focuses on this contingency in various ways. This may involve differential reinforcement of alternative behavior (e.g., a less maladaptive way of gaining attention), extinction of the target behavior (e.g., making sure to not provide attention when the maladaptive behavior does occur), or antecedent interventions (e.g., noncontingent reinforcement that provides attention on a time-based schedule). A function-based intervention may also be developed for behavior found to be maintained by the removal of instruction, as mentioned earlier. These interventions are designed to disrupt the prevailing contingency. For example, an intervention plan may involve teaching an individual to request a break or help in the presence of aversive demands. This plan may also include extinguishing the target behavior when it does occur (i.e., keeping instruction present despite the occurrence of the target behavior), as well as an antecedent intervention (e.g., offering choices to reduce the aversive context of the instructional situation). There are several benefits to looking at behavior in this way, particularly when one considers the implications of the mentalistic alternatives that flourish throughout the helping professions. These mentalistic alternatives all end up blaming the individual for their behavior in one way or another.

A Critical Analysis of the FBA Model

The interbehavioral field construct is distinguished from the operant contingency, and the general FBA model, in fundamental ways (chapter 3). Most importantly, the interbehavioral field takes no one variable to be more causal or influential than any other. This is to be contrasted with the operant-based FBA model, where the search for reinforcers is of the utmost importance, as those reinforcers are assumed to be causally responsible for the occurrence of the behavior. We want to note two things here: 1) remember, the operant model is a move in the right direction, a move away from mentalistic views of behavior that end up blaming the individual for their behavior, and 2) unfortunately, the FBA model encourages the assessment and analysis of a very specific range of factors, specifically the variable assumed to be the cause of behavior (i.e., the reinforcer). What's more, the FBA model even encourages a look toward very specific categories of reinforcers. These often include social attention, access to tangibles, escape from demands, and so on. It seems unlikely that researchers involved in this work initially intended for the model to become as ritualized as it is, but this does indeed seem to be the outcome (note that this particular issue seems to be a source of debate among researchers in this area; see Hanley, 2012).

While the conceptual concerns with the FBA model (and indeed operant psychology more generally) are serious on their own (Hayes et al., 1997; Fryling & Hayes, 2011), they are associated with a number of practice issues as well. Clinicians often find themselves dealing with challenging clinical situations even when the FBA model is carefully implemented. In our experience it isn't uncommon to hear a clinician describe how well-planned interventions, implemented with high levels of integrity, addressing functions identified in a thorough FBA, still fail to produce meaningful outcomes. That is to say, in the world of practice an operant perspective may not be sufficient to result in desired clinical outcomes. As we have suggested, the entire operant model is based on a confusion of constructs derived from basic research with the events that we are interested in (chapter 3). While this confusion is present in various areas of the discipline, it becomes rather glaring for clinicians engaged in practice. Indeed, if there is any area of behavior science that demands the recognition that the subject matter of interest is complex, multifactored, nonlinear, and dynamic, it is the area of clinical practice. Clinicians know this better than anyone; it is the experience of their day-to-day work in the field. Clinicians are working with the subject matter directly, with the primary aim of understanding idiosyncrasies in individual repertoires, and to facilitate the development of those repertoires in meaningful ways.

As we described in chapter 4, the field orientation emphasizes the participation of interbehavioral history and setting conditions. They are not considered mere things that support or strengthen a reinforcer. Rather, these factors are seen as important in their own right. Thinking this way may lead clinicians to consider factors such as a client's social life, interpersonal or social skills, and access to opportunities to develop these skills, before jumping to a more common FBA-based intervention as described above. For example, it could be the case that the "attention-maintained behavior" has nothing to do with a contingency whatsoever. Perhaps there is something else present or absent from the interbehavioral field related to the client's concerns and goals. Thinking of the broad context of the client's life, we might wonder whether the client has access to social opportunities, available and interested caregivers, or is involved in the community more generally. As one might imagine, this could have significant implications for therapy and intervention planning. Again, here we are shifting away from the narrowness of the contingency construct and considering our analysis from the perspective of the psychological event (i.e., interbehavioral field).

Similarly, a behavior considered to be maintained by "escape from task demands" may also be looked at differently from an interbehavioral perspective. Considering the historical and situational context in which the behavior is occurring, we might consider the extent to which the individual is prepared to complete the task being asked of them. For example, in a school setting it seems plausible that the child may not have the prerequisite skills to complete the task, and so the intervention might focus more on academic tutoring. Alternatively, it's possible that the student is not sleeping well and comes to the academic setting particularly tired. Or perhaps the physical setting itself is distracting; maybe it is crowded and noisy. We might also wonder whether the people involved in the setting are generally supportive and kind, or whether their behavior is contributing to the aversiveness of the setting. As you can notice from these examples, embracing a field perspective encourages one to think about the therapeutic context more broadly, to take a more interbehavioral field-based approach than traditional operant constructs tend to promote.

The topic of assessment is foundational to clinical work from a behavioral perspective. More than assessment in other areas, behavioral assessment serves to guide the development of intervention. While the FBA model helped turn attention to the environment rather than blaming the individual for their behavior, it is limited in that it encourages a focus on a narrow range of factors. Conducting assessment from an interbehavioral field-based perspective encourages the consideration of a larger range of factors and may inform more comprehensive intervention planning.

The following section considers the area of behavioral consultation, a practice area relevant to the work of many behavioral clinicians.

Behavioral Consultation

Another area of practice for behavioral clinicians involves consultation. This is not surprising, as the behavioral perspective places emphasis on understanding behavior as it occurs in the natural environment. This emphasis follows from more general philosophical assumptions, especially assumptions related to the rejection of dualism (chapter 1) and the assumption that behavior is not determined by something within the individual. In other words, behavior is functionally related to factors that participate in the situation where the behavior occurs, and not to hypothetical constructs within the individual. As behavior occurs in the natural environment, in the lives of the clients consultants work with, it is often in the clinical interests of the client to involve individuals who participate in that context in therapeutic efforts. An area in which this stands out is the assessment and intervention for challenging behavior, where the training of parents, caregivers, teachers, staff, and others can have a large impact on clinical outcomes. We now consider how the topic of consultation and training is approached in mainstream thinking, operant psychology, and finally, from an interbehavioral perspective.

Most approaches to training assume that teaching and training others involves a teacher (in this case a consultant) passing along information (in this case to the consultee). This is to say, developing knowledge is the aim of most training efforts. The assumption here is that once an individual has the knowledge required to complete an activity, they will then use that knowledge to carry out the task. In the area of intervention for childhood behavior problems, this may involve telling a caregiver or teacher about an intervention strategy, perhaps also providing a written set of instructions describing what to do. This way of conceptualizing teaching is at odds with behavioral thinking, and behavior analysts have found it to be insufficient to produce behavior change on the part of consultees. While the traditional way of teaching is limited, it is especially so when we consider training people to develop skills as opposed to more content-based instructional aims.

Behavioral clinicians working in this area have improved upon training practices by focusing on the skills of the consultee. Much of the research in this area focuses on a training package that has become known as behavioral skills training (BST), which, in addition to providing some information about the intervention, involves a consultant modeling the intervention, a consultee rehearsing the intervention, and the consultant providing feedback as to the accuracy of implementation (e.g., Kirkpatrick et al., 2019). Research in this area has consistently shown that consultee implementation of behavior intervention plans is improved when the skillful behavior of the consultee is the focus.

Still, clinicians working in the field know well that training a consultee to competency using a BST model, while important, is often not sufficient to make a lasting impact on the behavior of the consultee. In the previous chapter we noted how the reliance on BST likely comes from an assumption that poor implementation is a result of a consultee's skills or performance deficits (Fryling, 2014). In other words, that the consultee either doesn't know how to implement the intervention or that there is insufficient reinforcement to sustain accurate implementation. While this may be the case on some occasions there are other circumstances where this view can be quite limiting.

Recall that behavior is a participating factor in a complex, multifactored interbehavioral field, and as such, it seems plausible that there may be other factors to consider if a consultant is faced with chronic nonadherence to behavioral intervention plans. For example, a consultee could have difficulty implementing the intervention accurately because they are exhausted. Alternatively, there may be competing demands in the household, such as other children present who also require the attention of the consultee. Or perhaps the consultee does not have a supportive work environment where the intervention is to be implemented. All of this is to say, when thinking about all of these and potentially other factors that may be present in the interbehavioral field, interventions aimed at improving consultee implementation of behavioral intervention plans may shift. For instance, we may consider connecting a parent to a parent support group, or explore access to respite care of some sort, to help plan for a break, and more. Though these are just possibilities, they highlight the departure from the assumption that poor implementation is a result of a skills or performance deficit alone.

Similar to the previous section on assessment, there are many good things to highlight related to the traditional behavior analytic thinking in this area. One of the greatest contributions of behavior analytic work to the area of behavioral consultation is the shift away from focusing on the consultee's knowledge and toward the behavior of the consultee. At the same time, many clinicians have encountered situations where the BST model is insufficient. In our view it would be more useful for clinicians to begin with an interbehavioral perspective, and develop even more contextual, comprehensive, and individualized intervention plans from the outset.

The final section of this chapter focuses on the area of behavioral psychotherapy, and emphasizes how the interbehavioral perspective might be of use in this area of practice.

Behavioral Psychotherapy

We focus on two examples of how interbehavioral thinking may have implications for behavioral psychotherapy in this chapter. First, we will consider the topic of using evidence-based practices and the longstanding concern over a divide between researchers and clinicians in this regard. We then shift to how an interbehavioral lens may be useful in the ongoing assessment of clinical problems in a traditional therapy context.

Using Evidence-Based Practices

Many readers of this text are likely to be familiar with the longstanding divide between research and practice. While there could be less of a divide in practice communities that are more oriented toward science in general, there is still a difference between what is happening in the world of research and what is occurring in the day-to-day practice of therapists. We believe the interbehavioral perspective can help conceptualize this divide in such a way that the values and interests of both the scientific and the practice communities are understood and appreciated. Importantly, while there has been considerable emphasis placed on the value of research to inform practice (i.e., closing the research to practice gap), we will underscore the importance of *practice informing research,* and how this is also fundamental to the development of a comprehensive science of psychology. To start, we consider the research context.

What Is Research?

What is considered research differs across the various disciplines and fields within the sciences and humanities. What research is may range from qualitative methods more common in the humanities to the various quantitative approaches that are more common in the natural sciences. Within behavior science, the majority of the research uses quantitative methods. We believe this is likely owing to a philosophical emphasis on prediction and control in traditional behavioral thinking. And indeed, within the world of evidence-based practice, the focus is often on prediction and control (or "influence"). That is, research that establishes practices as being evidence-based is focused on understanding the extent to which a particular intervention works in resolving a particular problem.

Still, we have not yet considered the disconnect between researchers' findings and clinical practice. The disconnection likely has to do with the research process and the requirements for conducting high-quality research. For one, the sort of research we are talking about is often focused on studying a particular intervention, so we can learn about the relationship between the intervention and a measure related to the behavior of interest or particular issue. Still, in order to say something about that intervention, and clearly articulate what is functionally related to the change in behavior, we must be able to clearly describe exactly what that intervention is. For this reason, the intervention must become rather specified in research experiments and there must be strict protocols that are followed in a particular manner: First you do this, then you do that, and so on. Practicing clinicians are likely to say that this isn't how it goes, though. Things don't follow a linear progression in practice. The job of the clinician is much more complicated than this. Something happens, there is progress, there is a setback, and so on. There is an immediate tension between that which is being studied and how things actually unfold in a therapeutic context.

Another part of the research context is the requirement to answer the question of "for whom?" In other words, researchers need to say for whom the intervention worked (or didn't work), and what their presenting problems were. This requires researchers to be rather specific in their inclusion criteria. Participants need to have particular characteristics, and importantly, also not have other characteristics (e.g., maybe a participant can have one diagnosis, but not another, and only if they haven't done X, Y, or Z in the past two years). This is to say, the research process requires researchers to not only be very specific and rigid with respect to what their intervention is, but also with whom their intervention is being studied. This requirement is also quite unlike the context of practice, where clinicians are working with individuals who have diverse and complex histories, fall in between and across various diagnostic categories, and more. We mention only some of the ways in which research is distanced from the world of practice here. Our aim in addressing this is to bring some sense of understanding to the gulf between research and practice.

In summary, much of what intervention research gives us is an understanding of how some techniques work when applied in a particular way with a particular group of people.

It should come as no surprise that there is a disconnect between the research enterprise and the needs of practitioners, even those who are more scientifically inclined. This isn't to say that research is *flawed* or shouldn't be pursued. Actually, as suggested by Kantor (1953), research is fundamental to any scientific system (chapter 4). What we are saying, however, is that it is important to recognize the limitations of research. What happens in the context of an investigation is not to be confused with the events of interest. In what follows, we elaborate on the therapeutic context in which clinicians work.

The Therapeutic Context

To further understand the topic of using evidence-based practices, we consider the therapeutic context in some detail. As previously mentioned, while the techniques studied in research may be packaged in a particular step-by-step manner, the lives of the clients therapists work with are unlikely to unfold in such a way. To begin, the clients therapists work with are likely to have widely varying histories, histories that operate in the present moment in different ways. As such, a therapist who prefers to use a handful of techniques early on in developing a therapeutic relationship may find that these techniques don't work as well with all clients. Moreover, clients' histories continue to evolve and participate in the presence or absence of different substitute stimulus functions (e.g., memories, feelings). Practitioners are required to attend to how clients' histories are present in therapists' current interactions with them, and how these histories are always changing (including histories with the therapist; also see Sandoz, 2020, for more on this). Whether or not, and how, various evidence-based practices are used effectively in the therapy context must be sensitive to unique and distinctive features of the ever-changing individual histories of clients.

History is one thing participating in the therapeutic context, and the large range of setting factors is another. Therapists are likely to be familiar with situations where a change in a setting factor completely changes the course of therapy. Life is complicated and circumstances can change in a moment. For example, a therapist may be working with someone who discovered their partner has been having an affair. Or someone may be offered the job of their dreams, which involves an incredibly high amount of stress in addition to more money. By contrast, losing one's job could also change the entire field in which therapy is ongoing. Car accidents happen, people become ill, they recover, and more. Therapist factors are relevant as well. For example, a therapist may have a more or less trusting, therapeutic relationship with a client, and this relationship may serve as a setting factor for the entire therapeutic context (indeed, there is much research on this particular setting factor). Sensitivity to setting factors necessitates a recognition that life is complex and constantly changing, and life-changing events are not confounds that can be eliminated.

We have highlighted interbehavioral history and setting conditions in this chapter to underscore the differences between the therapeutic and research contexts. From our perspective, the field construction of interbehavioral psychology helps elucidate the disconnect between research and practice. Research is important, but how findings from research are incorporated into the complexities of a practice setting is an entirely different issue. The interbehavioral field construction may also help clinicians as they conceptualize their cases and troubleshoot when progress is lacking. Moreover, while we have been considering the relationship of research to practice, there is also a practice to research relationship to consider. In our view, the experiences and challenges of practitioners point to important issues to explore in behavioral research, and considerable attention should be focused on eliminating the disconnection between practice and research. This gap is not only large but also overlooked entirely at times.

We conclude with some general thoughts about approaching clinical work from the perspective of the interbehavioral field. As behavior therapists it is always important to remember, first and foremost, that individual attributes aren't the causes of behavior. This may be especially important to remember in a traditional psychotherapy context, where all that is physically present is the client (i.e., causes are hard to point to). Assuming that behavior is a function of the historical and situational environment is an important first step, a step that traditional constructs in behavioral thinking encourage as well. But traditional constructs seem to take us only so far. Clinicians may find their practices ineffective when they are constrained by contingency models. It is important to remember that traditional constructions, while they may be helpful in particular contexts, are not the events of original interest. The events of original interest to practitioners are more complicated, as we have described in this chapter.

Summary and Key Points

This chapter reviewed a number of implications of the interbehavioral field construction for the practice of behavior analysis. This included the topic of behavioral assessment and a detailed analysis and critique of the functional behavioral assessment model. Our review of assessment was followed by a critical analysis of function-based interventions. Particular areas of practice were also addressed, including behavioral consultation and behavioral psychotherapy. Evidence-based practice was also considered. This included a discussion of the nature of research and the need to consider the context more thoroughly in applications of behavior analysis. Interestingly, given these considerations, practitioners may be more likely to understand that the subject matter of behavior science is an interbehavioral field.

Study Questions

1. Explain how the FBA model is derived from linear, operant-based foundations.
2. Comment on the strengths and weaknesses of the FBA model from the perspective of interbehaviorism.
3. Provide an example where an interbehavioral perspective might shift the focus of an intervention.
4. How is consultation considered from mainstream/mentalistic, traditional behavioral, and interbehavioral perspectives?
5. Describe some of the issues in the section on the disconnect between research findings and clinical practice.
6. Give two examples of circumstances where interbehavioral history and/or setting factors are critical to understanding a hypothetical therapy context.

Part 2

Theoretical Applications

Part I of this text provided an introductory overview of some of the foundations of the interbehavioral position. Throughout part I, we tried to strike a balance between describing Kantor's work and our interpretations of it along with its implications for the development of the behavioral perspective. Part 2 of the book focuses on extensions of interbehavioral thinking. Some of the chapters in this part pertain to topics that Kantor has specifically addressed (e.g., memory), others reflect our own extensions of interbehavioral thinking (e.g., relationships), and still others are a hybrid of Kantor's work and our extensions upon it (e.g., inapparent events). This is to say, we are not simply reviewing Kantor's work, but rather providing our own analyses of various topics addressed by Kantor, along with how they might be applied to matters of interest to contemporary behavior scientists.

While many aspects of Kantor's work have influenced our extensions, the concept of stimulus and response substitution (chapters 3 and 6) is fundamental to almost all of it. The distinction explicitly acknowledges the difference between the physical and psychological properties of events that, in turn, eliminates the need for speculation about nonnatural phenomena (e.g., mind, psyche). In other words, failing to acknowledge this distinction, in mainstream psychology as well as in behavioral circles, contributes to the persistence of dualistic and reductionistic thinking in behavior science. Further, this absence contributes to long-held concerns that the behavioral position isn't fully comprehensive (Kantor, 1970). Generally speaking, what makes the analysis of stimulus substitution and implicit responding so helpful is that these constructions facilitate the analysis of complex events in which the stimulus, response, or both are not apparent to the observer (see Hayes, 1994).

Part 2 of the book includes chapters on psychological linguistics (chapter 6) and inapparent events (chapter 7). We then shift to related topics, including memory (chapter 8), perspective-taking and relationships (chapter 9), feelings and emotions (chapter 10), and human development (chapter 11). Each of these chapters examines unique extensions of interbehavioral thinking involving stimulus substitution and implicit responding. Finally, the last two chapters, on family values (chapter 12) and morality (chapter 13) build upon Kantor's analysis of cultural behavior. While these topics are not exhaustive, they point to the range of topics to which an interbehavioral analysis might be applied.

CHAPTER 6

Linguistic Behavior

The behavior of humans is distinguished from that of nonhumans by the engagement of the former in what Kantor (1982) calls cultural behavior. As linguistic behavior is the dominant type of cultural behavior, we think it important to begin our discussion of linguistic behavior by describing the category of cultural behavior to which it belongs.

Cultural and Noncultural Behavior

Kantor (1982) distinguishes several categories of behavior on the basis of their time of development, mode of origin, and distribution across the human population. Among these categories are those of the universal, basic, suprabasic, and cultural types. To distinguish cultural from noncultural behavior, we need only compare cultural behaviors to those of the universal, basic, and suprabasic types. This is the case because behavior of the universal and basic types is noncultural, while actions of the suprabasic type include both noncultural and cultural behaviors. We describe the universal, basic, and suprabasic categories in more detail below.

Behaviors of the universal category include simple responses observed in neonates (Kantor, 1924). They are stimulated initially by things touching the surface of the organism as well as by conditions within the organism itself. Over a relatively short period of time, more distant objects become available through auditory and visual stimulation. Included in the universal category are elementary reflex responses. Reflex responses are ahistorical in the sense that they do not evolve into different forms by way of repeated exposures to stimulus objects. Neither are they explicitly trained. They simply occur as an adaptation of the organism's biological characteristics to the physiochemical properties of stimuli. They are distributed universally, which is to say, all humans engage in acts of this type.

As organisms begin to have movable contacts with environing things, behavior of what Kantor (1924) calls the basic and suprabasic categories develop. Actions of these types are not reflexes but rather adjustments to the natural properties of environing things (for the most part). Early on we observe reactions of the "protective, defensive, expressive, exhibitive, and other modes of adjustment" (Kantor, 1982, p.5). More elaborate forms of these behaviors develop over continued contacts with environing things. Behavior in these categories is not distributed universally though, because the breadth of an individual's basic and suprabasic repertoires depends on the number and kinds of stimuli with which the individual has been in contact. Further, some of the stimulus functions operating in these types of behavior segments do not have their sources in the natural properties of stimulus objects, but rather in attributed properties. This is to say, actions of basic and suprabasic types include cultural actions, to which we now turn.

As an introduction to the topic of cultural behavior, Kantor states: "Cultural behavior is distinguished from noncultural behavior on the basis of the stimulus functions to which the reaction functions are performed" (1982, p.4). To clarify, the stimulus functions to which cultural reactions are performed do not have their sources in the natural properties of stimulus objects. Instead, they are performed with respect to attributed properties of stimuli. Their forms are thereby arbitrary. For example, the response "river" is not determined by the natural properties of a flowing body of water. This is to say, there is nothing about a flowing body of water that should give rise to the response form "river." As such, cultural responses cannot develop in the absence of explicit culturalization. Rather, cultural repertoires develop under the auspices of persons already responding in common ways to attributed properties of stimuli. The properties of stimuli have become institutionalized in this sense.

Obviously, the properties attributed to stimulus objects in one collectivity are not the same as those attributed to the same object in another. For example, in one collectivity a cultural action with respect to a flowing body of water is "river," while in another it is "río," in another "fleuve," or "fiume," and so on. What distinguishes one collectivity from another are the properties attributed to stimulus objects; how persons respond to those properties identifies them as members of a particular collectivity. Linguistic activity is an especially good example of this circumstance, as it is both the dominant type of cultural behavior and the means by which the attribution of stimulus properties is accomplished.

As just mentioned, properties of stimuli are attributed to them by way of linguistic activity. We will address this issue in greater detail below. For now, we presume that the practice of attributing properties to stimuli has been happening throughout the entire evolution of societal groups, that its origins and development are coincident with the organization of human society. By this we mean that the attribution of stimulus functions by linguistic action and the organization of human groups happens coincidentally, neither preceding, following, or being responsible for the other. Over the course of societal evolution, responses, stimuli, the properties of each, and all other factors are "named," and their names are shared and meaningful within groups and unfamiliar and meaningless across them (Parrott, 1984).

We are reminded at this juncture of Skinner's refinement of the definition of verbal behavior (Skinner, 1957, pp.224–25). His strategy in this regard was to consider the behavior of the listener, and he concluded that it is only when the response of the listener has been conditioned "precisely in order to reinforce the behavior of the speaker" (p.225) that the behavior of the speaker could be considered verbal. He further argued that the special conditioning of the listener in this regard is conducted "precisely to create a means of control" (p.225). We mention Skinner's thoughts on this issue not because we share his views about reinforcement, but rather because both he and Kantor (1982) talk about linguistic practices as agents of social control. While we recognize that groups are held together in large part because of their linguistic practices, we do not agree that they act as agents of social control for the reasons presented above. Moving on, we turn to an examination of Kantor's views on the topic of psychological linguistics more generally.

Linguistic Interbehavior

Kantor's work on the topic of psychological linguistics appears in two books (1936, 1977) and many papers published over the period from 1924 to 1983 (see the appendix). Among these papers are approximately fifty published under his nom de plume, "Observer" or "Mitsorg."

Accordingly, his work on this topic is too extensive to be fully detailed in this chapter. Instead, we will focus on just the two main types of linguistic behavior discussed in these works, namely referential and **symbolic behavior.** According to Kantor (1936, pp.73–75; 1977, p.80), the fundamental distinction between these two types of linguistic behavior is that **referential behavior** is bistimulational and symbolic behavior is serially stimulational. Before we compare these two types of linguistic activity (including what is meant by bistimulation and serially stimulation), we focus briefly on what these two types, as members of the linguistic category, have in common.

•

Conventionality of Form. Linguistic behaviors of both the referential and symbolic types are cultural in kind, as described above. They are conventional forms of responding, occurring with respect to attributed properties of stimuli, acquired under the auspices of group circumstances. Linguistic response forms are thereby arbitrary. Nonlinguistic responding bears a different relationship to stimulus objects. Response forms of nonlinguistic actions are conditioned by the natural properties of stimulus objects, including their size, shape, weight, and so on. The forms of nonlinguistic responses are therefore not arbitrary.

Conventionality of response form is not a property of linguistic action exclusively. However, linguistic action differs from other kinds of behavior in this regard in that every instance of linguistic behavior has this property, while some instances of nonlinguistic action exemplify nonconventional responding. This feature of linguistic action affords possibilities for great variation in form (see Parrott, 1984, 1986b).

.

Indirectness of Action. When responding operates directly upon a stimulus object, such as to change its location in space, we may call the action direct. For example, we act directly upon a coffee cup when we pick it up. Much of a person's nonlinguistic behavior is direct in this sense, though not all of it. For example, behavior of the feeling type does not act upon environing stimulus objects but rather upon the responding organism (see chapter 10). Also, nonlinguistic actions are indirect when relevant sources of stimulation are absent, as when a person sees something in its absence by way of substitute stimuli operating from nonoriginal sources. This is to say, in the absence of a sandwich, a person can see it (indirect action), but not eat it (direct action). As a point of contrast, Skinner (e.g., 1957, 1974) failed to distinguish between stimuli as objects and stimuli as functions. As such, when responses occurred in the absence of relevant stimulus objects, he was forced to conclude that responding could occur without stimulation.

Unlike nonlinguistic behavior, linguistic behaviors of both the referential and the symbolic types are examples of indirect action. Linguistic behavior does not act directly upon environing objects such that those objects are modified, destroyed, relocated, or otherwise changed. Linguistic action is indirect, and this is the case even when it is occurring with respect to stimulation inhering in immediately present stimulus objects.

As previously mentioned, Kantor (1936, 1977) partitions the category of linguistic behavior into two main types, referential and symbolic, the former being bistimulational, the latter serially stimulational (e.g., Kantor, 1977, p.80). These types are described below.

Referential Interbehavior

In ordinary language, referential behavior is a case of one person (a speaker) acting in such a way as to orient another person (a listener) to some environing thing or event. In technical terms, the act of orienting another person is called "referring," and the thing or event to which the other person is oriented is called the **"referent."** The speaker is called the **"referrer,"** and the listener is called the **"referee."** In Kantor's terms, then, referential behavior is a case in which a referrer refers a referee to a referent. Henceforth, we will use these technical terms. Unlike in all other varieties of psychological events, where interactions involve one response function interrelated with one stimulus function, linguistic actions of the referential type are bistimulational (Kantor, 1936, 1977). Bistimulation describes a circumstance in which one response function is interrelated with two stimulus functions operating from different sources at the same time. From the referrer's perspective, one source of stimulation is the referee, the other is the referent. Integrated with this interaction, and occurring simultaneously, is action of the same bistimulational sort occurring on the part of the referee. For the referee, one source of stimulation is the referrer, the other is the referent. In both cases, the referent is termed the **adjustment stimulus,** while the person serving as a source of stimulation in such segments (the referee for the referrer and vice versa) is termed the **auxiliary stimulus.**

A referential segment is not just a matter of one person acting in such a way as to make it possible for another person to be oriented to some environing thing. The other person must, by this action, be oriented to that thing. That is, when the referrer reacts linguistically to a snake on the path, the referee likewise reacts to the snake. The acts of the referrer and the referree are held to occur simultaneously (Kantor, 1977, p.71). Of importance here is the fact that, for Kantor, the actions of both the referrer and the referee in a referential segment are linguistic in kind.

Kantor's position is at odds with Skinner's (1957) in this regard. Skinner overlooks the linguistic actions of the listener (i.e., listening and understanding) in favor of the listener's nonlinguistic acts of mediating consequences for the speaker's behavior (see Parrott, 1984, for further explanation). Also overlooked by Skinner is the particularity of the listener as a stimulus. He argues that "an adequate account of verbal behavior need cover only as much of the behavior of the listener as is needed to explain the behavior of the speaker" (Skinner, 1957, p.3). It is as though any listener will do. Not so, however as the particularity of the listener ends up being important enough to give rise to the construction of the audience variable.

There are exceptions to the character of a referential segment as described above. As Kantor (1977) explains, in some circumstances the referee, as a source of stimulation, is absent. We sometimes talk to people in their absence. For example, a person may say goodnight to a picture of a loved one. The absence of the referee as a source of stimulation does not mean that the stimulus functions of the referee are absent. It means that these functions are operating from another source, in this example, the picture. In other words, the auxiliary stimulus function is substitutional. Obviously, though, if the referee is not physically present in a given behavior segment, neither are his/her actions of listening and understanding.

Sometimes it is the referent that is missing. We talk about things that aren't present. The same analysis applies here, namely that the stimulus functions of the adjustment stimulus, in this case, are operating from another source object. They are substitutional. Still, in both instances, the referential segment is bistimulational.

As Kantor (1977, p.68) puts it: "Referential behavior pervades the entire psychological life of the individual. There is first the great universe of discourse which includes conversation ranging from the most trivial gossip to the discussion of the weightiest problems of politics, art, business, and science." Added to these, he mentions acts of mutual aid and morality taking place in collective circumstances, as well as acts self-communing (i.e., talking to oneself), that operate in acts of reflecting and decision-making.

Linguistic behavior of the referential type is further clarified by examining its connections with nonlinguistic behavior. In this regard, Kantor (1977) draws a distinction between **narrational** and **mediational** segments. Mediational segments are those in which referential behavior is closely connected with nonreferential behavior. A typical case is one in which a referential interaction results in a nonreferential interaction, as when one person asks another to close the door and the second person does so. (Events of this sort are what Skinner, 1957, calls "mands.") The nonreferential action mediated in this way may be quite subtle. This is the case when the referential behavior mediates a nonreferential action of the perceptual type as when, for example, the referrer orients the referee to a sunset, and the nonlinguistic action of the referee is just to see the sunset.

These examples illustrate cases of mediation in which the referential action precedes the nonreferential action. In other cases of mediational segments, the nonlinguistic behavior accompanies the referential action. Kantor (1977, p.70) supplies an example of this case as when a mother (the referrer) tells her child (the referee), while they are gardening together, that the child has planted a straight row. While the referential action in such cases does not in itself bring about the nonlinguistic adjustment of planting straight rows, Kantor suggests that "her remarks may prove very effective in mediating a more successful adjustment on the part of the child" (1977, p.70). Given that mediational segments are those in which referential action is closely connected to nonlinguistic action, referential action may also follow nonlinguistic action. The linguistic action in such cases has no effect on the nonlinguistic action that has already been completed. It is included in the mediational category simply because of its close relation to nonlinguistic activity.

Finally, in some circumstances the referrer is unable to perform the nonlinguistic action called for under those circumstances. Kantor (1977, p.71) exemplifies this circumstance with the case of a man who sees his blown-off hat sailing down the street and cries out, "My hat! My hat!" In such cases, because the nonlinguistic action of retrieving the hat cannot occur in the ongoing segment, linguistic action substitutes for it. This exemplifies the case of response substitution as described above.

As previously mentioned, referential segments of the mediational and narrational sorts are distinguished by their relations with nonlinguistic action. We have been discussing mediational segments. Narrational segments, by contrast, are those in which referential behaviors have no mediational functions whatsoever.

Recall that Kantor partitioned the category of linguistic behavior into two main types, referential and symbolic. He claimed that the difference between them had to do with their stimulational circumstances, with referential behavior being bistimulational and symbolic behavior being serially stimulational. We turn now to the case of symbolic behavior.

Symbolic Interbehavior

Symbolic behavior is an important category in Kantor's analysis of psychological linguistics.

We consider varieties of symbolic behavior in detail below.

Simple Symbolic Interbehavior. In simple symbolic behavior, the actor is said to be interbehaving with a symbolic situation taken as a whole. For example, when responding to the identity of ♀ and saying the word "female," a person is interacting with an inseverable couple. Though ♀ and female are numerically two things, they constitute a single stimulus object inasmuch as only one stimulus function inheres in the couple. Such interactions are, in principle, exactly like the nonlinguistic actions discussed in the previous section of this chapter. As Kantor (1977, p.76) puts it: "The simple symbolic behavior segment is therefore not a unique form of psychological interbehavior since we cannot justifiably differentiate behavior classes on the basis of the type of object with which the reactor interbehaves." Unlike some types of nonlinguistic activity, the typical simple symbolic segment always involves a substitute stimulus function. Again, as a point of comparison, Skinner (1957) differentiates various classes of verbal behavior, including the echoic, textual, and tact, among others, based on the type of object to which the person responds.

Complex Symbolic Interbehavior. Complex symbolic behavior is a unique form of psychological behavior. Kantor (1977, p.77) makes a point of saying that unlike the case of simple symbolic behavior, in which a person is interacting with a symbolic situation, complex symbolic behavior takes place within in a symbolic segment. The point he is making is that in a complex symbolic segment there are two (or more) distinct stimulus objects, each with its own stimulus function. Unlike the case of referential behavior, in which responding with respect to the stimulus functions of the axillary and adjustment stimulus object occurs simultaneously, contacts with the functions of stimulus objects in a complex symbolic segment occur in sequence.

The segment in this case is composed of two phases. In the first phase, contact with the first of these objects takes place. Operating from this source is a substitute stimulus for the adjustment stimulus of the completed interaction. The product of immediate action with respect to stimulation from this source (i.e., the act of recognizing the stimulus object as a symbol) serves as the second stimulus object in the sequence. In the second phase, acting with respect to the stimulus function of the second object amounts to saying, knowing, or otherwise responding to what the symbol stands for. An example of this sequence of events would be one in which the first stimulus is °√16.

Responding with respect to the function of this stimulus would entail reaction systems of attending and discriminating, culminating in an awareness that √16 is a symbol. Operating from this source is a substitute stimulus for the adjustment stimulus of the completed interaction, namely "4." More complex symbolic situations involve a longer series of substitutions. It is important to note here that it is only the action of the referee (i.e., the listener) that can be brought into relation with symbolic activity. This stands in contrast to behavior of the referential type, where actions of both the referrer and referee are involved.

We began the discussion of referential and symbolic behavior by distinguishing them on the basis of their stimulational conditions, with referential behavior being bistimulational and symbolic behavior being serially stimulational. This is the fundamental difference between them from which other differences arise. One such difference is that referential behavior is a factor in an immediate adjustment. This is to say, the referrer's stimulus function does not point to a subsequent orientational contact with another object. As such, the question as to what the referrer's stimulus stands for never arises: It does not stand for anything (Kantor, 1977). In a symbolic segment, by contrast, an object's stimulus function leads to another orientational contact with the stimulus for which it stands.

Another difference between referential and symbolic behavior has to do with their connections to nonlinguistic behavior. As previously discussed, referential behavior is intimately integrated with nonlinguistic behavior, while symbolic behavior is far removed from other behavior. From this perspective, contemporary investigations of linguistic behavior, including research on stimulus equivalence and relational frames, exemplify behavior of the symbolic type in which only listeners are engaged.

Listening and Understanding

Linguistic activity is a part of pretty much everything human beings do—so much so that some have conceptualized linguistic behavior as the medium of contact between linguistically competent people (e.g., Ribes, 2020). All complex forms of human activity, including such acts as thinking, remembering, and problem-solving, are accomplished by way of linguistic activity. As such, we are obliged to analyze more than just speaking and listening. Rather, we need to consider listening with understanding and speaking with meaning. Meaning and understanding are not conceptualized by Kantor and Skinner in similar ways, and given that we suspect that the readers of this text are more familiar with Skinner's analysis of verbal behavior than with Kantor's analysis of psychological linguistics, we will attempt to clarify Kantor's position on these issues by comparing it to Skinner's position.

Listening and Understanding from a Radical Behavioral Perspective

Skinner (1957, pp.357–67; 1974, pp.141–47) did not fail to address the concept of understanding, although his views on this issue are not well integrated with his views on verbal behavior (Parrott, 1984). For example, understanding is not even mentioned until the tenth chapter of the book *Verbal Behavior,* and a functional analysis of the concept suffers further delay. Still, he does address this issue, and we may examine his views. Actions of understanding what a speaker has said are conceptualized by Skinner as varying from engaging in basic echoic responses, to responding with respect to a situation in an appropriate way, to understanding which factors influence a speaker's response (i.e., why they are saying what they're saying). This analysis is not without its problems, however. In the first place, as Parrott (1984) points out, to identify understanding reactions with echoic behavior is neither conventional nor valuable. As she puts it, "Making an echoic response to verbal stimulation in an unfamiliar language is not what is ordinarily meant by the term 'understanding' and no useful purpose is served by reducing a complex phenomenon to a simpler one and then changing the meaning of the term to accommodate the simpler phenomenon" (p.30). Likewise, to conceptualize understanding as "appropriate behavior" does not facilitate an understanding of understanding,; it merely identifies this event with another more obvious activity on the part of the listener, namely, reinforcement meditation.

Finally, Skinner's most complex form of understanding is conceptualized as knowing something about the controlling variables for an instance of verbal behavior. An assessment of Skinner's analysis of this type of understanding requires us to consider what knowing means in this context. A review of Skinner's treatment of the concept of knowing reveals a number of distinctly different interpretations (Parrott, 1983b); however, the most common interpretation is that knowing is acting (Skinner, 1974, p.138).

Knowing as acting is subdivided into three types based on the complexity and multiplicity of the response topographies involved. The simplest kind of knowing implies little else than contact with stimulating conditions. To "know," in this sense, means to be intimate or familiar with a set of circumstances (Skinner, 1974, p.138). The second kind of knowing as acting is "knowing how to do things." By inference, a more complex response form is involved in this case. Further, a single topography or collection of topographies, related to a given set of circumstances, is involved. What one knows in "knowing how" is what one does (Skinner, 1969). This sense of knowing does not seem to carry the meaning implied by his definition of knowing being something about the controlling variables for the speaker's behavior. Rather, it seems more closely related to Skinner's intermediate level of understanding, that is, "knowing how" is synonymous with understanding interpreted as "responding appropriately." And, in the context of the listener's response to verbal stimulation, responding appropriately means mediating reinforcement for a speaker's behavior.

The third form of knowing as acting is what Skinner calls "knowing about" (1974, p.138). It is this form of knowing that we believe is implied in Skinner's concept of understanding. According to Skinner, then, to know something about the controlling variables for an instance of verbal behavior, in other words, to understand what a speaker has said, "means that one has acquired a relatively large number of different responses under an equally large number of variant circumstances in which these controlling variables have played a significant part" (Parrott, 1984, p.31). To understand is to be able to respond in multiple ways.

This analysis is relatively satisfying, and it is quite conventional. One problem remains, however. What we have here defined as "understanding" does not constitute some current performance. To understand or to know about, as here conceptualized, refers to a behavioral repertoire, not an instance of behavior. In other words, what Skinner seems to be talking about is not knowing per se but knowledge. According to Skinner (1953, p.409; 1974, p.138, p.142; 1978, p.105), knowledge is whatever a listener is capable of doing. In his words, "It is potential behavior which is called knowledge," (1974, p.363). Note, however, that "potential" behavior is really nothing at all until it becomes actual behavior, in which case knowledge, from the standpoint of an instance of its occurrence, is nothing more than whatever it is a listener does in response to verbal stimulation. In other words, knowing, as well as knowledge, amounts to the same thing: reinforcement mediational activity.

Reinforcement mediational phenomena are probably focused on by Skinner because these are the only observable aspects of the listener's involvement in a verbal episode. Both listening and understanding would be "private events" in Skinner's analysis, and therefore they may only be inferred on the basis of overt behavior that is assumed to occur after, and be dependent upon, prior listening and understanding (i.e., the idea being that the behavior wouldn't have occurred if the individual didn't engage in some listening and understanding). And reinforcement mediation is one such overt performance. Focusing on something overt and measurable may be necessary for the purposes of research, but it is not necessary for conceptual analysis—and moreover, Skinner's analysis of verbal behavior is a conceptual analysis. Hence, in our view, his neglect of listening and understanding as contemporaneous activities is indefensible. The fact that listening and understanding may be subtle events doesn't mean they cannot be studied (more on this in the next chapter). Neither does it diminish the significance of their participation in linguistic segments. It simply calls for a different type of analysis than is required of reinforcement mediational activities.

Listening and Understanding from an Interbehavioral Perspective

As alluded to above, an analysis of language requires a conceptualization of both listening and understanding. We begin with listening, followed by the more complex concept of understanding.

•

Listening. From an interbehavioral perspective, listening is conceptualized as all psychological events are, as a function obtaining between the responding organism and the stimulating of environing features. Listening events are also historical and always changing over the course of an individual's lifetime. As such, any particular listening event is to be considered the present point in the development of previous instances of listening (Parrott, 1984). Given this, when someone is listening, they aren't just responding with respect to an auditory stimulus, but also to their entire history with respect to that stimulus. A sound isn't just a sound. This is why a poorly executed vocalization of the person's name, while unintelligible to someone with a less extensive history of hearing this sound, is heard by the person as their name. The current sound, because it bears some similarity to historical occurrences of the sound of the person's name, and because it partially substitutes for them, stimulates listening responses of previous forms. As such, listening responses are aspects or phases of a composite form that includes the poorly executed vocalization in the present circumstance.

As these sorts of perceptual happenings involve both current and historical factors, Kantor and his students (Kantor, 1924, pp.295–315; Kantor & Smith, 1975, pp.198–201; Pronko, 1980, pp.382–86) have referred to them as *semi-implicit*. In their account, a current stimulus participates in two functions, one direct or explicit, the other indirect or implicit. The explicit function is simply the relationship obtaining between the auditory stimulus as it occurs in the present moment and the hearing reaction coordinated with it. The implicit function involves substitute stimulus functions derived from an individual's previous interactions with the stimulus. Staying with the above example of a poorly articulated name, someone may hear a name by way of implicit functions, even when the name wasn't actually said (explicit functions). Here, the partial explicit functions participated with the implicit functions (hence being "semi-implicit"). These historical reactions combine with the reaction stimulated by the sound in its poorly executed form, producing a composite, and novel, response (Parrott, 1984).

As Hayes (1992b) has pointed out, this analysis facilitates a conceptualization of the past as present. Indeed, current perceptual interactions *involve* an individual's history of perceptual interactions. There is no other place where past interactions may exist, no storage of the past or changed organism to carry the past into the present (chapter 8). Perceptual behavior, like all behavior, only occurs in the present.

In conclusion, the behavior of listening is not given adequate consideration in Skinner's analysis of the verbal episode. The neglect of listening in Skinner's formulation reflects his positivistic and operationistic biases. Discussions of the processes by which we come to "tact" so-called private events substitute for technical descriptions of such events in Skinner's system. His analysis of thinking (1957, pp.432–52) and of private events in general (1945, pp.270–77; 1953, pp.257–82; 1974, pp.21–32) exemplify this strategy. The apparent privacy of listening renders it subject to the same circumvention. More specifically, verbal reports of having listened substitute for an account of the actual events of listening in Skinner's analysis. The two are not synonymous, however, and a complete account of a verbal episode must include an analysis of listening per se, as we have tried to provide.

•

Understanding. Understanding is similar to listening in that it too consists of a functional relation between the linguistic stimulation and the responding of a listener. Understanding is also historical, with each instance of understanding comprising the individual's history of responding with respect to similar stimuli. Still, listening and understanding are not the same. Listening reactions are less complex relative to understanding reactions. Understanding reactions do not occur in nonverbal organisms; understanding what a speaker has said is something only a verbal organism is capable of doing.

A great deal of implicit responding is involved in understanding reactions, making them incredibly complex. Recall that in the simpler case of listening, it was argued that current auditory stimuli brought about historical listening reactions as a matter of current stimuli substituting for themselves at earlier times. The substitute stimulus functions involved in listening reactions develop as a result of current auditory stimuli sharing some similarity with previous auditory stimuli. This is one way substitute stimulus functions develop, but there are other arrangements that facilitate stimulus substitution. Spatiotemporal relationships of all sorts may serve as association conditions that later participate in substitute stimulus functions and implicit responses. Auditory stimuli often occur in spatiotemporal proximity to other stimuli, such as visual stimuli. We see dark clouds and then hear rain, for example. Later, when we hear rain alone, we may imagine dark clouds, even if we aren't looking out the window to check whether they're there. From an interbehavioral perspective, we say that the auditory stimulus of the rain is substituting for the seeing of the dark clouds. Note that there is nothing similar between the sound of rain as a stimulus and the dark clouds as a stimulus. The substitute stimulus functions developed in this example as a result of a history of spatiotemporal proximity between the sound of the rain and the sight of the clouds (Kantor also refers to these as conditions of association; Kantor, 1924).

All of this is to say that it's not just the history of responding with respect to a particular stimulus that participates in an individual's perceptual behavior; it's also all of the *other* responses they have engaged in within spatiotemporal proximity to perceptual behavior. Moreover, the fact that all of these historical interactions are present in any particular occurrence of understanding adds to their complexity. (For further understanding of these and related issues, see Parrott, 1984, 1986b; Hayes, 1992b.)

From the speaker's perspective, the object of a verbal episode is to induce a listener to respond in various ways. Further, it is often in a speaker's interest to induce a listener to respond with respect to stimulus objects that are not immediately present. For instance, a listener may be asked to fetch something missing from the current situation, or to imagine, plan for, or otherwise react to circumstances yet to occur. In such cases, it is incumbent upon a speaker to produce substitute stimuli for the listener, as it is only with respect to such stimuli that these reactions on the part of the listener may be expected to occur. A speaker may not be sufficiently familiar with a particular listener's history to select a workable substitute, however. Yet, the inability of speakers to select workable substitute stimuli for unfamiliar listeners has not served to restrict communicative interchanges of this type to only the most intimate of friends. On the contrary, it has led to the development of highly conventional associations of stimuli—objects and the arbitrary patterns of auditory or visual stimulation known in the vernacular as their "names."

As a result of this development—that is, the development of language—speakers are able to induce listeners to react to things and events in their absence, and it is this activity on the parts of listeners that may be called "understanding what the speaker has said." Parrott (1984) explains that understanding is seeing, touching, hearing, or otherwise responding with respect to actual things and events in the presence of their names alone. Moreover, understanding is a complex event involving historically associated happenings. These actions may be very subtle in their operation and may have a partial or vestigial character. They occur nonetheless, and their occurrence may be explained by appeal to the frequent coordination of verbal and perceptual events throughout the behavior lives of individual listeners. In sum, from an interbehavioral perspective, understanding what a speaker has said is not usefully interpreted as a repertoire of potential behavior. It is, rather, a unique, contemporaneous response of the listener with respect to the stimulation produced by a speaker's behavior in the present moment.

All of this points to a need for further conceptual analysis, including the full range of factors that participate in language events. Indeed, one of the hallmarks of productive sciences is their comprehensiveness—their attempts to address all aspects of their subject matters. If we are to cultivate a throughgoing and vibrant science of behavior, then we must be willing to extend our analytical and investigative methods to all behavioral events regardless of the problems they present for observation.

Summary and Key Points

We have described the processes of stimulus and response substitution that are operative in all instances of linguistic and other forms of complex interbehavior. We have described the two main types of linguistic behavior identified by Kantor and have contrasted his analysis with that of Skinner. Finally, we have made an analysis of listening and understanding as contemporaneous actions in the interests of fostering a more comprehensive coverage of the subject matter of behavior science.

Study Questions

1. Distinguish between cultural and noncultural behavior.
2. Define referential behavior. Be sure to include the concept of bistimulation in your answer.
3. In your own words, distinguish between referential and symbolic behavior.
4. Distinguish between mediational and narrational segments of referential behavior.
5. Provide an example of both simple and complex symbolic behavior.
6. Explain the interbehavioral interpretation of both listening and understanding.

CHAPTER 7

Inapparent Events

As discussed in chapter 1, interbehaviorism is a technical philosophy pertaining to individual disciplinary sciences as well as to natural sciences more generally. It consists of definitions and postulates articulated at different levels of scope. Interbehavioral psychology, as a natural science, is founded upon and formulated in terms of this philosophy. As such, the definitions of its subject matter and the premises concerning it are extended, without contradiction, from definitions and postulates articulated at levels of greater scope (Kantor, 1958). To put it another way, the philosophical assumptions of interbehaviorism as a philosophy of science extend to the discipline of psychology, including how the subject matter of the science of psychology is constructed (chapter 3). This pattern of relations assures the internal consistency of a scientific system that, in Kantor's (1958) view, constitutes a measure of its validity (chapter 2). A valid system is one in which constructions concerning events at levels of lesser scope—in this case, the subject matter of a natural science of psychology—are consistent with those pertaining to constructions concerning events at higher levels of scope, namely those pertaining to natural science as a whole.

One benefit of a valid system is the guidance it provides for the formulation of obscure or particularly complex psychological events such as thinking, remembering, and problem-solving. Characterizing events of these sorts requires a greater degree of theoretical and methodological extension than is required for more apparent and less complicated phenomena. For this reason, the characterizations of these events are especially vulnerable to unbridled construction (see Parrott, 1983c, 1986a; Hayes, 1994). Indeed, we are more likely to make conceptual errors or fall into the convenience of traditional ways of thinking when we are attempting to analyze these more complex1 events. In Kantor's view, "Nowhere in the entire field of psychology has the evil of simplification and abstractionism struck with such force or culminated in such disaster as at the point of thinking, problem solving, and reasoning" (1926, p.201). In our view, the bifurcation of psychological events into private (inner) and public (outer) categories exemplifies this disaster.

The bifurcation of psychological events in this way violates the standards of internal consistency (again, see chapter 2). For example, psychological systems of the behavioral type have claimed the actor in a psychological event to be the whole organism, not its parts considered separately (e.g., Skinner, 1953). Nonetheless, a subset of such events, namely those of the "private" class, are held to be enacted by special parts of organisms, such as the brain (Skinner, 1953, 1957, 1969, 1974). Likewise, behavioral systems tend to acknowledge that there are no responses without stimuli, no stimuli without responses, yet several varieties of psychological events are held to constitute responses in the absence of stimuli, among them perceptual and intellectual acts of all sorts (e.g., Skinner, 1957, 1974). Further, stimuli are sometimes said to be "ineffective," which, given the premise of no stimuli without responses, is nonsensical.

There is a lack of consistency in how behaviorists have conceptualized these events. In our view, these inconsistencies are owing to a lack of adequate systemization in behavior science (see Parrott, 1983c), including the absence of specific assumptions concerning its subject matter. The effect of these inconsistencies has been to thwart investigation of events relegated to the private class (see Hayes & Fryling, 2009a), and, in so doing, shrink the purview of behavior scientists to something less than the events historically isolated as the subject matter of psychology. The effect has been to undermine the claim to a comprehensive science, one that provides a coherent analysis of all events that fall within the scope of the subject matter. This is to say there have been both conceptual issues and related practical problems associated with the traditional practice of referring to complex psychological events as being private.

Disciplinary sciences that develop and evolve through the process of system building, including the rules of noncontradiction across levels of construction, are valid. Interbehavioral psychology is a valid system aiming to achieve a high level of comprehensiveness. As such, it is obliged to formulate complex events in such a way as to maintain the internal consistency of the larger scientific system and, importantly, to enable events of these types to be contacted and investigated.

System Constraints

Before attempting to characterize events deemed too complex and/or obscure to be investigated, we must be reminded of the definitions and postulates of the larger system of which events of these types are continuations—the specific postulates of interbehavioral psychology (chapter 3). Among them are contentions that psychological events involve actions of whole organisms and that the events of one science are not reducible to those of another science (Kantor, 1958; see chapter 3). Hence, even the most obscure psychological phenomenon cannot be conceptualized as being enacted by a part of the organism, including a “master” part, because psychological events can’t be reduced to biological events. The brain is a biological organ. Thinking is a psychological event. Brains don't think; people do. Further, a psychological event is conceptualized as an interdependent relation of responding and stimulating taking place in a multifactored field (Kantor, 1958). Such events are held to originate and evolve over the course of an individual's lifetime, whereby the way persons act with respect to stimulation depends on the ways they have previously acted under given conditions.

With this understanding as to the nature of psychological events, our task becomes one of developing a strategy for how we might observe and investigate the most obscure varieties of these events. In this regard, we may be reminded that psychological events constitute unique occurrences in the sense of intimacy and fleetingness (Kantor, 1958). This means that a psychological event, as an interaction of a particular response of a particular individual with a particular stimulus in a particular setting, occurs once and only once (see Hayes, 1994). This is to say, all psychological events are unique events. With regard to matters of intimacy and fleetingness, we may take intimacy to mean that, at a given time and place, a particular person with a particular history was involved. By fleeting, Kantor (1958) notes that psychological events are transient processes of brief duration. Any analysis of psychological events is aided by clarifying the particularly unique features of the subject matter. (As we mentioned in chapter 3, readers may also be interested in Fryling & Hayes, 2009, for more on the unique features of psychological events.)

Accordingly, the construction of particular types of psychological events, such as thinking, reasoning, or problem-solving, must proceed from this starting point. Acts of these sorts have common as well as distinguishing features. As for their common features, these acts are what Kantor (1926, p.119) calls "non-effective" in character. This means that the stimulus objects from which coordinate stimulus functions are operating are not manipulated, transformed, or otherwise changed by their performances. These types of responses are also alike in that their response forms are largely inapparent to observers (Kantor, 1926, p.119), meaning that their performances lack significant participation of skeletal and muscular reaction systems. In this regard, intellectual responses, including thinking, reasoning, and problem-solving, are subtle. Added to these commonalities, intellectual responding is largely implicit, meaning that it is occurring with respect to substitute stimulation.

Nonetheless, actions categorized as being particularly complex and obscure are able to be distinguished one from the other by examining the factors participating in their occurrences. Recall that psychological events from an interbehavioral perspective consist of multifactor fields (chapter 3). These factors, along with their organization, vary across event types. For example, Kantor (1926, p.148) describes thinking acts as "a series of behavior segments which result in a person's intimate interaction with situations and objects so that operations upon them are very effective or feasible" while "problem solving, as the name implies, consists primarily in overcoming difficulties and problematic situations" (1926, p.148). Kantor distinguishes multiple types of intellectual responses, such as believing, doubting, opining, convincing, and hypothesizing, in this same way (see Kantor, 1926, pp.119–45). Added to the unique configuration of factors by which the various classes of obscure and particularly complex events may be identified is the even more specific configuration present when a particular person with a particular history engages in such behavior. That is, it is important to remember that each psychological event is a unique happening.

Inapparent Stimulation and Responding

As previously discussed, from Kantor's perspective, psychological events may be both complicated and subtle, but they aren't private. Like all other psychological events, they take place in multifactored, integrated fields. They are, as such, able to be observed and investigated. We turn now to these issues specifically.

From our perspective (Hayes, 1994; Hayes & Fryling, 2009a), psychological events present observational problems when responses, stimuli, or both are not configured in such a way as to serve as a stimulus for an observer. Responses may be inapparent because skeletal and muscular reaction systems are not prominent features of their forms. Acts like thinking present a problem of this sort, even if the stimuli with which such responses are coordinated are immediately obvious. For example, we may know that a person is thinking about some particular thing but not what they are thinking about it. Likewise, the stimuli with which responding is coordinated may be inapparent because they are substitutive, as when a person reminisces about the past. Such acts are problematic even if their response phases are immediately apparent. This is to say, we may observe overt memorial actions—for example, talking about one's family member who passed away—but not the stimulus circumstances with which they are coordinated such as to have been actualized at this time.

As these two examples show, there are times when we may know what the stimulus is but not what the response is due to the response being subtle (as in the previous example of knowing that a person is thinking about some particular thing, but not what they are thinking about it). At other times, the response may be apparent, but not the coordinated stimulus due to its being substitutional or, in some other way, obscured. Both circumstances present observational challenges. Even more challenging are subtle acts of thinking or remembering occurring with respect to substitute stimulation.

Observing as a Psychological Event

Observing is the means by which events of all types are drawn into scientific consideration (Kantor, 1953). Observing operations are fundamental to science. Nonetheless, observing is a psychological event. As such, from an interbehavioral perspective, it must be conceptualized as a function "obtaining between the responding of a whole organism and the stimulating of some aspect of the environment, set in a field of many other factors" (Hayes & Fryling, 2009a, p.51). Hayes and Fryling (2009a) further suggested that "while each such event is unique, each is also an historical accumulation of prior occurrences in which those particulars were participating factors" (p.51).

Given that observing events on the part of individuals are cumulative in this sense and that no two individuals have the same histories of observing, what one person sees on a particular occasion is not what another person sees. (Indeed, it is not even what the same person sees, as a person's history is constantly evolving and therefore what a person sees now is different from what was seen in the past.) All of this is to say that acts of observing are not unbiased. Further, it is our contention that not all events are able to be observed in the same way, which we will address in more detail in what follows.

Observation of Events Involving Inapparent Stimulating

In the case of apparent responses occurring with respect to inapparent stimulation (e.g., talking about something that happened at a previous time), we cannot suggest that such responses occur in the absence of stimuli, as has been suggested by Skinner (1974), for example, because this interpretation does not comport with our definition of psychological events as a relation of responding with respect to stimulation. Instead, identifying the source of stimulation for such a response is the conceptual problem to be solved. In these instances, the source of stimulation for this response cannot be the events that happened at a previous time, as these events are no longer physically present to serve in this capacity, whereby responding must be assumed to be coordinated with substitute stimuli. As discussed elsewhere in this text (chapters 3 and 6), substitute stimulus functions develop when multiple stimulus objects and their functions occur under conditions of association for a given individual such that the functions of one object may come to operate from other sources for that individual at another time (i.e., one of the objects present during those initial association conditions may come to develop the stimulus functions of another present object).

Observation of the stimulus phases of behavior segments involving inapparent stimulation depends on the observer's knowledge of the stimulus objects that might be harboring the substitute stimuli operating in the present environment. In other words, observing inapparent stimulation depends upon the extent to which the observer shares the history of the initial association conditions that may have participated in the development of current substitute stimulus functions. Sometimes source objects may be assumed on the basis of typical organizations of stimulus objects, as when two individuals who are frequently together (e.g., good friends) substitute for one another, and vice versa. This is to say some sorts of association conditions are not a part of a more intimate history, whereby it may be relatively easy to observe the inapparent stimulation occurring. When one member of a couple shows up to a party without their significant other, someone may ask, "Where's your partner?" and the substitution occurring may be relatively obvious to anyone who is familiar with the couple.

Observation of inapparent stimulation of a more idiosyncratic sort, the sort that we are probably most interested in when we consider an analysis of thinking, depends on an intimacy of the observer and the observed, however. Hayes (1994, p.159) explains, "To the extent that an observer knows how a particular individual is stimulated by immediately *obvious* stimulus objects—a knowledge accumulated over the course of many interactions between the two persons—that is the extent to which the observer knows which objects serve as substitute stimuli for that particular individual." Knowing what serves as a source of substitute stimulation is what observing means in such circumstances. This sort of knowledge may constitute a sort of shared history, whereby the observer may also respond to the inapparent stimulation to which the observed is responding (more on this in chapter 9).

Thinking about an individual with whom you have a long and/or intimate relationship may help clarify some of these issues. You might identify many sources of substitute stimulation for an intimate friend, in part because you respond to substitute stimulation inhering in the same sources. Thus, a shared history with another person permits you to detect the substitute stimuli present. Those with a lesser relationship may detect the presence of stimuli with substitute functions to a lesser extent, and those who share very little might not notice any source of substitute stimulation. Our point here is that the degree to which one has knowledge of inapparent stimuli has nothing to do with those stimuli being private, but rather with the extent to which an observer has had a relationship with the person interacting with the functional properties of the present stimuli.

Observation of Events Involving Subtle Response Forms

Our definition of a psychological event also prevents our taking the position that some responses are impossible to observe because they are taking place in locations that are inaccessible to observers (e.g., minds, brains, or otherwise "private" locations). This won't solve the problem because all psychological events are held, from an interbehavioral perspective, to be taking place in the same location, namely, in an event field. Remember too that reducing these events to biological happenings violates the postulates of a natural science of psychology from an interbehavioral perspective, specifically that psychological events cannot legitimately be reduced to the events of another science, and that psychological events involve the responding of the whole organism (Kantor, 1958, see chapter 3).

Considered independently of stimulation for analytical purposes, a response may be conceptualized as a sequence of biological reaction systems, including those of the glandular, muscular, and skeletal types, among others. This sequence culminates and configures as a response of the psychological type (Kantor, 1958). Responses differ as to the types of organismic systems comprising their response forms, and these differences impact observers differently (see Hayes & Fryling, 2009a). Responses of subtle form are not unobservable in principle, though. As with inapparent stimulation, the observation of subtle responses depends on the intimacy of the observer with the observed. An observer familiar with a person's overt actions with respect to apparent stimulation may be able to observe more subtle actions coordinated with these stimuli than an unfamiliar observer. Again, the capacity to observe inapparent events is a matter of shared history.

Thinking about a good friend may help understand our main points again here. While in the previous section we noted that an observer's ability to detect inapparent stimulation is dependent on the intimacy of their relationship with the friend, in this section we are talking about inapparent responses. A person (A) with an intimate relationship with another person (B) might notice a range of subtle responses with which Person B is engaged. Person A might notice that Person B is upset or excited about something, for instance. Subtle responses may be aspects of a more overt pattern previously witnessed. This to say, a history of observing the subtle actions of another person depends on their shared history. Someone with a less intimate history may not recognize the character of the friend's subtle activity, or even that such activity is ongoing. In short, the greater the shared history of two persons, the more readily observed are their subtle responses to each other.

While we have distinguished between inapparent stimulation and responding in this chapter, it is often the case that both are happening—that both inapparent stimulation and subtle responding are occurring at the same time. These circumstances are especially vulnerable to dualistic constructions. In other words, in the absence of apparent stimulation and responding, one is more likely to invoke hypothetical mental events and processes to explain such phenomena as thinking and problem-solving. Given the aims of a natural science of behavior, this is exactly what we wish to avoid. The present chapter provides an alternative to mentalistic understandings of these sorts of subtle psychological events.

Summary and Key Points

Interbehavioral psychology aims to provide an account of all events that fall within the subject matter of psychology, including some of the most complex psychological happenings. These include thinking, reasoning, problem-solving, remembering, and more. Conceptualizing these events in a manner that is consistent with the definitions and premises of the scientific system more broadly is especially challenging when these aspects of the system are not explicit. Complex events may come to be articulated as private responses in the absence of stimuli (e.g., Skinner, 1953), by which their investigation cannot be pursued. From an interbehavioral perspective, complex events of these sorts are public events available for investigation. In the chapters to follow, we will build upon the issues in this chapter, as they address some of the most socially important and complicated psychological events.

Study Questions

1. What are the implications of the distinction between public and private events in behavior science as it pertains to system building as described in chapter 2?

2. Describe some assumptions of interbehavioral psychology, especially those pertinent to a consideration of inapparent events.

3. Provide an example of a psychological event involving inapparent stimulation.

4. Describe an example of a psychological event involving both inapparent stimulation *and* implicit or subtle responding.

5. What are the systemic implications of the analysis in this chapter? What role, if any, do supposed private events have in a natural science of behavior?

more broadly is especially challenging when these aspects of the system are not explicit. Complex events may come to be articulated as private responses in the absence of stimuli (e.g., Skinner, 1953), by which their investigation cannot be pursued. From an interbehavioral perspective, complex events of these sorts are public events available for investigation. In the chapters to follow we will build upon the issues in this chapter, as they address some of the most socially important and complicated psychological events.

Study Questions

1. What are the implications of the distinction between public and private events in behavior science as it pertains to system building as described in chapter 2?
2. Describe some assumptions of interbehavioral psychology especially those pertinent to a consideration of inapparent events.
3. Provide an example of a psychological event involving inapparent stimulation.
4. Describe an example of a psychological event involving both apparent stimulation and implicit or subtle responding.
5. What are the systemic implications of the analysis in this chapter? What role, if any, do supposed private events have in a natural science of behavior?

CHAPTER 8

Memory

This chapter is devoted to the topic of memory, elaborating upon our previous work in this area (Fryling & Hayes, 2010, 2014). We dedicate a chapter to this topic not only because it is interesting but also because many practical problems are related to the topic. Sometimes the problem is that people have difficulty remembering events of the past. They may not recall what happened a week ago, yesterday, or even earlier in the day. On the other end of the spectrum, it may be the case that people can't seem to forget something that happened, be it a traumatic event, an argument with someone, or a missed opportunity. The incident may seem to be present in their lives no matter how much time has passed. In lay terms, we might say that the problem is they can't forget. Issues related to memory can go both ways.

There is also the common instance of remembering that is remembering to do something in the future. So much of our lives is consumed by setting up various reminders, developing planners and calendars, and so on. While this topic has implications for day-to-day life and overall life self-management, it also pertains to serious issues such as taking care of one's health, diet, and more. It is easy to see how the topic of memory is pertinent to many issues of daily living, and also that there are different types of memory.

Finally, and even more fundamentally, the topic of memory is closely related to the topic of learning. Situations in which the term "learning" is used typically involve a circumstance in which a particular behavior is not found to be occurring in a specific situation, followed by some sort of teaching, training, or therapy with respect to that behavior. Then, at some later time, a demonstration of that behavior having been learned is made. Relevant to our consideration of memory in the present chapter, we might say that learning involves someone "remembering what they had previously learned."

The topic of memory has far-reaching implications for the analysis of many types of socially important behavior. Further, memory calls attention to the fundamental assumptions of different psychological formulations. In the following section, we provide an overview of different ways of thinking about memory from both a more traditional behavioral perspective and a mainstream psychology perspective. We take issue with these approaches to the topic from the standpoint of the postulates described in part I of this book. This will set the stage for an alternative interbehavioral approach to memory, which is the focus of the chapter.

Traditional Approaches to Memory

Before we explain particular theories of memory, we want to identify an underlying task, or challenge, encountered in the formulation of all such theories. In short, all instances of memory involve time in one way or another, and theorists are thereby obliged to explain how something of the past, some experience or learning, is made present in the current psychological context. (Or, as we would say, how it is that the past participates in the present psychological event.) Most theories in psychology involve some version or combination of dualistic and reductionistic ideas, and theories of memory are no exception. In what follows we provide a brief overview of dualistic and reductionistic theories of memory. We also consider how the behavior analytic theories approach the topic.

Dualistic Theories of Memory

Throughout this book we have been calling attention to the distinction between approaches to the subject matter of psychology are derived from contacts with events (natural science approaches) and those derived from more traditional, dualistic folklore. All dualistic theories have one thing in common—they attempt to explain something contacted in the natural environment, such as thinking about a past experience, by pointing to something that has not been confronted in any way by anyone. In the area of memory, dualistic ideas follow some version of this logic: An individual has some experience in the world, that experience is copied and stored in their mind or psyche, and then at some later time, they are able to remember the past experience by consulting the stored copy of it. More modern forms of this same logic are presented in computer metaphors.

Reductionistic Theories of Memory

Reductionistic theories of memory are not unlike dualistic theories. While the logic is the same, the storage facility is different. In these theories, copies of experiences are stored in the brain. That is, an individual has an experience and that experience is then said to change the individual's brain in some way. Upon some later occasion, the brain is activated in such a way as to retrieve the stored copy whereby the individual remembers the experience. Reductionistic theories also speculate about different types of storage facilities. Some have to do with time, as when copies of experience are said to be held in short-term facilities while others occupy long-term facilities. Some bins hold copies of experiences related to spatial relations. Some are said to be working, others not. The reductionists' invocation of brain sections as storage facilities as opposed to the hypothetical facilities proposed by dualists appears to render the former's theory of memory the more naturalistic of the two—at least as long as the proposed brain sections are not themselves hypothetical. Large bodies of research have focused on identifying different areas of the brain that seem to be associated with different sorts of remembering (more on this below). Still, the logic is the same: It is assumed that experiences are somehow held in individuals, and that at some later time memory occurs as a result of these experiences being called up from storage in some way.

Behavior Analytic Theories of Memory

Behavior analytic theories of memory depart from dualistic and reductionistic theories in some important ways. Most obviously, behavior analytic theories of memory focus on the behavior of memory and factors associated with increasing or decreasing the occurrence or frequency of memorial behavior. There is a specific aim to move away from dualistic storage metaphors in behavior analytic thinking (e.g., Marr, 1996), with more of a focus on how memory may be improved with practice and behavioral intervention (e.g., Delaney & Austin, 1998), including how memory may be viewed as a special case of problem-solving (e.g., Palmer, 1991; Skinner & Vaughn, 1983). In this sense, traditional behavior analysis bypasses our initial challenge somewhat, there is relatively less emphasis placed on explaining how past experiences of an individual come to influence the present, and more emphasis is placed on practical issues.

Still, behavior analysts have tried to explain memory. Interestingly, when behavior analysts attempt to explain how an individual's past experiences are brought into the present moment, a familiar pattern of suggesting those experiences have been stored in some way shows up. Behavior analysts suggest that the individual is changed in some way through their experiences (Skinner, 1974). For example, when explaining the topic of memory, Skinner states, "The contingencies which affect an organism are not stored by it. They are never inside it; they simply change it" (1974, p.121). A similar analysis is made with respect to perception, where Skinner (1974, p.93) states, "A person is changed by the contingencies of reinforcement under which they behave; they do not store the contingencies." These comments seem to suggest that learning more fundamentally may be explained by way of a changed organism. While notions of a mind or psyche are avoided, as is a specific focus on the brain, there is a focus on the individual as a biological organism being changed in some way, and that this changed individual is the means by which the past is brought into the present. In this sense, at least at the level of explanation and conceptual analysis, the behavior analytic approach seems similar to the dualistic and reductionistic approaches. Something happens, it is somehow taken in by the individual and changes the individual in some way, and at a later time the individual engages in memorial behavior because the individual has changed and is presumably a different person.

Philosophical Concerns

Recall from chapter 1 that our interbehavioral aims are focused on developing a natural science approach to the analysis of behavior. Natural science approaches are distinguished from dualistic approaches in that hypothetical entities are avoided, particularly as they may be invented to be causes of behavior. Given this, dualistic theories that employ the mind, psyche, or even some metaphorical computer as a means of explaining memory are dismissed as incongruous with the overarching aims of interbehaviorism.

Reductionistic theories are also problematic. This is not because the brain isn't important to an understanding of psychological events. Rather, focusing on the brain as an explanation for memorial behavior doesn't provide an explanation for this type of behavior from the standpoint of a natural science. Rather, it provides a neurological analysis of a psychological event. The brain (as well as the rest of the organism) participates in a psychological event, but it does not explain it. That is, whatever areas of the brain are held to be participating in memory, including different sorts of memory, do not themselves, alone or in combination, constitute a description of the psychological event of remembering, much less explain it. We can't neglect the task of providing a psychological analysis of memorial events by substituting a biological analysis for them.

Further, studies of the brain often sustain an element of dualism. What's new in these theories is the nature of the storage facility. No longer are memories stored in hypothetical mental facilities; instead, they are stored in a confrontable bodily organ. This is a step in the right direction. The next step in this direction, as we see it, ought to be to abandon the storage and retrieval metaphor. All of this is to say that something else is worth considering, something that provides a psychological analysis of memory from a natural science perspective.

The Interbehavioral Approach

Kantor's analysis of psychological events allows for a valuable alternative to the aforementioned conceptualizations of memory. We begin with the issue of time as a fundamental feature of any understanding of memory.

Time and the Psychological Present

Earlier we noted how all theories of memory are obligated to deal with the topic of time. That is, an analysis of memory requires us to consider how the past is influencing the present situation, how something that is no longer here (i.e., the past) is somehow still here. Moreover, addressing the topic of remembering calls for consideration as to how we project things into the future, the sort of remembering to do something that we described at the beginning of the chapter. Both the past and the future are constructions of time, and time is even more fundamental than the past and the future in an understanding of memory.

The interbehavioral approach to time differs from the dualistic, reductionistic, and behavior analytic interpretations mentioned above. Building upon the interbehavioral field construction, which includes the interbehavioral history and the substitution of stimulus functions (chapter 3), we understand time to be a construct that is used in the present, with both the past and the future to be considered aspects of the present situation. That is, when someone thinks about the past, they are interacting with present substitute stimulus functions of stimulus objects in the current environment. They aren't interacting with the past as something that is distinct from the present but rather with the past as the present. Similarly, when someone thinks about the future, they are thinking about a constructed future, a constructed future that exists in the present moment. All psychological happenings involve only the present psychological event, and derived from this is the observation that the future, like the past, cannot be distinguished from present happenings. If we go back to our fundamental challenge for all theories of memory, for dealing with time and more specifically to account for how the past is brought into the present, the challenge is dissolved by our interbehavioral approach. There is no time other than the present, and we therefore no longer need to explain how the past is brought into the present because they are one and the same. This topic is addressed in a seminal paper by the first author, titled "The Psychological Present" (Hayes, 1992b).

For example, from this perspective, when an individual thinks about someone from the past, they are engaged with the present environment. Sometimes it is obvious what they are interacting with, what part of their environment is the source of the substitute stimulus functions of their past in the present psychological event. Looking at your high school yearbook is an obvious example of this. While doing so, it is likely that someone will do more than interact with the direct stimulus properties of the pictures and text on the pages. The pictures and text are likely to have a great many substitute stimulus functions (e.g., remembering a class you took, how funny someone was). As this example makes clear, the individual looking at their yearbook isn't interacting with the past as something distinct from the present environment; they are interacting with the past as part of the present.

This analysis is sufficient and consistent with our natural science aims. There is no need to infer a hypothetical mind or psyche, nor is there a need to attribute psychological action to brain activity. Other times, the source of the substitute stimulus functions is less clear. There are countless situations where someone remembers something from the past and doesn't know why it showed up at a given moment. Inasmuch as psychological events are multifactored interbehavioral fields, it is oftentimes not possible to isolate the object source of the substitute stimulation actualized in a memorial event. Moreover, the actualization of a function from this source is taking place in setting of many factors, all of which are participating in the event. Thus, a memorial event occurs in an integrated field. It is not a product of any aspect of that field in isolation. It is happening in a setting composed of many factors. We suspect that this not knowing what to point to, where to turn for an easy explanation of memorial events, may contribute to the persistence of dualistic theories.

Similarly, when someone projects something into the future (such as writing an appointment down in a planner), they do so with respect to a constructed future, and that constructed future is also present in the psychological event. That is, at the moment of interacting with one's planner at a later time, a person is interacting with an aspect of the present psychological event, just one that substitutes for a previous construction of the future. This notion, that the past and future are aspects of the present and therefore not distinguished from the present, seems to be particularly unique to the interbehavioral perspective.

Different Types of Memorial Interactions

We have referred to different types of memory throughout the chapter thus far. Our sensitivity to different types of memory is influenced heavily by Kantor's writings on the topic. Kantor uses specific terms to refer to different types of memorial events (Kantor, 1922; Kantor & Smith, 1975). In the next section we provide a brief overview of Kantor's distinctions between reminiscing, remembering, and memorizing interactions. We also include implications for research and practice, and in doing so, consider the topic of forgetting with respect to each of the types of memorial action described. As we mentioned at the beginning of the chapter, it is not always the case that our aim is to improve memory, and moreover, even when we do wish to improve it, we at the same time aim to reduce forgetting. In other words, a consideration of factors that participate in memory are, at the same time, always involved in an analysis of factors that contribute to forgetting.

Before we start reviewing the different types of memory, Kantor describes how all types of memory have three phases (1922; Kantor & Smith, 1975). The first of these phases involves initial association conditions whereby stimuli, settings, people, and more are associated in space and time. This is followed by the passage of some time (the second phase of memorial interactions), and then, finally, the third stage, where the memorial interaction occurs. While these three phases are aspects of each of the different types of memorial interactions, each of these types has distinctive features. We turn now to reviewing the different types of memorial interactions proposed by Kantor.

Reminiscing

We start with reviewing Kantor's analysis of reminiscing interactions. Reminiscing involves the three phases of all memorial interactions. First, there are initial association conditions, where various factors appear together in space and time, providing the conditions for the development of substitute stimulation. In the case of reminiscing interactions, these association conditions could involve almost anything: people, places, events, and even particular feelings. There is then some passage of time, and finally the individual interacts with a substitute stimulus, concluding the reminiscing interaction. Reminiscing interactions are distinct from the other types of memorial events in that they are decidedly *backward looking* in Kantor's terms. This is because the third phase of the memorial interaction involves a psychological event with some stimulus object that has acquired substitute stimulus functions derived from previous events.

Reminiscing interactions are quite common. For example, you may have had a rather intense meeting with someone you work with related to a particular project. After some time, you may be attending a separate work meeting where someone mentions the topic while reviewing things that the group is working on. The mentioning of the topic may have the substitute stimulus functions of the initial meeting where the topic was a source of tension, such that you think about that initial meeting as the topic is currently mentioned. More traditionally, we might think of an example of reminiscing that pertains to someone or some event from our more distant past. For example, if a child's grandmother always gave them bread with too much butter, they may think of their grandmother whenever they encounter bread with too much butter, even many years later. Here the initial association conditions involved the grandmother, the overly buttered bread, and the table where they ate the bread. Similarly, when driving through different areas of a city one might reminisce about things they have done in those areas, people they met there, and so on. In each of these examples, the reminiscing interaction is concatenated by a substitute stimulus developed in the past, maintaining the "backward looking" feature of reminiscing that Kantor describes.

•

Research and Application. Based upon our analysis of reminiscing, we suspect that many factors serve to promote or inhibit these types of interactions. For example, considering the first phase of the memorial interactions, namely the initial association conditions, the frequency of contact with these conditions may be especially relevant to the occurrence of reminiscence. Thus, the more often particular association conditions are encountered, the more likely they may be to sustain the substitutional functions enabling reminiscence. We also suspect that those who talk a lot about the past are likely to sustain and elaborate upon the substitute stimulus functions derived from the original conditions of association by doing so. It may be for this reason that those interested in preserving memories in the elderly have used memory wallets (i.e., a series of pictures related to the person's life) to stimulate conversation about the past (e.g., Bourgeois, 1992). By contrast, when the past is rarely or never discussed, reminiscing interactions with respect to those substitute stimulus functions may be less likely.

It also seems likely that the less often a particular factor has been involved in association conditions composed of other factors, the more likely are reminiscing interactions with respect to these conditions to occur. For example, if you have only one historical interaction with someone (or any particular factor), then reminiscing interactions with respect to that factor may be more likely to be preserved. By contrast, if many association conditions have occurred, many "memories have been created," then reminiscing interactions with respect to specific events may be less likely or may depend upon a very specific configuration of factors in any psychological event.

As mentioned above, there are also circumstances where reminiscing is problematic, such as when someone cannot forget the past. Here we suspect that developing new association conditions with respect to the stimuli participating in the reminiscing interaction would be beneficial. For example, it could be that forgetting about a difficult conversation at work would be facilitated by having other conversations about the topic, perhaps even with the person who was present during the initial difficult conversation. This may explain the therapeutic use of exposure and acceptance-based interventions that are popular in mainstream psychology. Although these interventions don't target forgetting per se, the overarching therapeutic aim is to diminish the reminiscing interaction in some way. By contrast, deliberate attempts to stop thinking about a particular incident are necessarily occurring in the old as well as new conditions of association, whereby the overall presence of the reminiscing interactions concerning this event may be enhanced rather than diminished. In other words, trying to forget may prevent forgetting.

Remembering

Like reminiscing interactions, remembering interactions involve the three phases of all memorial events from the interbehavioral perspective. Remembering interactions are unlike reminiscing interactions, though, in that they are *forward looking*. That is, remembering interactions involve "projecting something into the future," using Kantor's words (Kantor, 1922). Specifically, in remembering interactions, a description of activity to be completed at a later time is deliberately established as a substitute stimulus in the first phase. Following a period of time (second phase), the third phase occurs when the previously established substitute stimulus, describing the activity projected into the constructed future, is contacted. For example, in initial association conditions, a verbal substitute for an appointment at some time in the constructed future is established and noted in some way (e.g., in a calendar). Contact with the substitute stimulus at the previously projected time of its occurrence completes the remembering interaction. Forgetting occurs when the substitute stimulus is not contacted at the projected time for the appointment.

It is interesting here that while the remembering interaction is distinguished from reminiscing interactions in being forward looking, it is actually also backward looking. That is, when you are remembering, you are reminiscing about what you had previously planned to do in the future. We mention this because the past and the future are distinct in an interesting way. Specifically, while the past and future are both aspects of the present circumstance, there was a past that was experienced and is now present, whereas the future only exists as a verbally constructed point in time. There never has been a future that exists outside of present verbal constructions of it (Hayes, 1992b).

•

Research and Application. A number of things may enhance or diminish remembering interactions. First, there are things that may impact the initial association conditions. We might consider what was happening in the presence of the initial association conditions. We may wonder, did the individual actually respond with respect to those factors needed to project the event into the future? *How* was the response projected (i.e., what sorts of reminders/prompts/substitute stimuli were created)? Similarly, how complex were the initial association conditions? For example, "do x but only if y has happened, and z has not happened for X days," as in the case of monitoring and management of chronic health conditions. This circumstance could also be related to false positives, or remembering to do something but at the wrong time. For example, if there are many factors involved in the initial association conditions, as when a compound stimulus is involved, then any one part of that compound stimulus may later substitute for it. Still, if the remembering is only to occur when all of the factors are present, this may contribute to the occurrence of false memories more generally (Fryling & Hayes, 2014). All of these circumstances may interfere with remembering interactions.

Finally, factors present during the third phase of the remembering interaction may also disrupt remembering interactions. If many other activities are ongoing such that contact with the substitute stimulus doesn't occur at the appropriate time, then the remembering interaction can't be completed. Such is the case when a person forgets to do something because they are too busy. What does occur at any given time is a matter of the setting conditions at that time. Accordingly, when relatively routine setting conditions are not present, relatively routine interactions are disrupted. This may explain why a person on vacation forgets to take their routine daily medications.

Memorizing

We include memorizing because, while it is a certain type of memorial interaction, it is often assumed to be a model for all memorial interactions. Memorizing interactions do seem to fit with the general model of memorial interactions in that they involve initial association conditions, followed by a passage of time, and subsequently a demonstration of memorial activity. For example, we might learn another language by engaging in exercises that involve hearing certain words in the presence of particular stimuli (e.g., a picture of coffee while hearing the word "café"), and then saying "café" upon being prompted to do so. Interestingly, the initial association conditions in which memorial interactions of this sort take place involve the development of a new interaction. In this example, the new interaction is saying "café" in the presence of the prompt to do so and the picture of coffee. Memorizing is demonstrated when, upon a subsequent occasion, saying "café" occurs under different setting conditions and with respect to only partial stimulation relative to those present when the response was initially acquired (i.e., in the presence of only the picture of coffee). Importantly, for these responses to be examples of memorizing activity, they would need to be absent prior to the initial association conditions for their occurrence. More obvious examples of these initial association conditions might involve remembering where you parked in a parking garage—where you repeat "B4, B4, B4" with the expectation that these interactions will increase the likelihood of you engaging in the response "B4" when you come back to the lot.

As mentioned above, memorizing interactions involve developing a new behavior, and they are distinct from both reminiscing and remembering for this reason. Reminiscing and remembering interactions do not involve developing a new behavior with respect to a stimulus. Rather, they involve association conditions in which substitute stimulus functions are developed and subsequently reencountered. In memorizing, new responses are developed with respect to original stimuli and later demonstrated. For these reasons, memorizing interactions, while they may be amendable to investigation, are not good models for understanding the complexity of factors involved in reminiscing and remembering. Table 8.1 depicts the three types of memorial interactions.

Table 8.1. Reminiscing, Remembering, and Memorizing Interactions Compared

	Reminiscing	Remembering	Memorizing
Phase 1: Initial Association Conditions	Association conditions among factors.	Association conditions involve an act to be completed in the future and a time for the act to be completed.	Association conditions involve repeating new response in the presence of the stimulus.
Phase 2: Passage of Time	Passage of time	Passage of time	Passage of time
Phase 3: Final Interaction	Interaction with a present stimulus with substitute stimulus functions of an absent stimulus.	Interaction with a present stimulus that substitutes for the previous association conditions, whereby additional behavior may occur.	Demonstration of a newly developed action with respect to a stimulus.
New response developed?	No	No	Yes
Substitute stimulation involved?	Yes	Yes	No

Summary and Key Points

Memorial activity is an important topic with far-reaching implications for conceptual analysis, research, and practice. Our aim in this chapter was to present the interbehavioral alternative to more traditional conceptualizations of memory to encourage both researchers and clinicians to think about the topic in new ways. The chapter also serves to facilitate theoretical discourse in psychological science, and is consistent with our overarching aims of developing a natural science approach to the discipline of psychology. Kantor's differentiation of these three types of memorial activity aligns with other disciplines that have also identified distinct types of memory (e.g., prospective memory, retrograde amnesia) and may therefore also serve as a starting point for productive interdisciplinary work.

Study Questions

1. Compare and contrast dualistic and reductionistic theories of memory. What do they have in common, and what makes them distinct?
2. What are the strengths and weaknesses of the behavior analytic approach to memory?
3. Very generally, describe how the concepts of time and stimulus substitution pertain to the analysis of memory.
4. Distinguish between reminiscing, remembering, and memorizing interactions.
5. Why are memorizing interactions particularly poor models of study memory?

CHAPTER 9

The Self, Perspective-Taking, and Relationships

Like other chapters in part 2 of the text, the topics of the present chapter involve issues of day-to-day living. This chapter addresses how we conceptualize and come to know ourselves and others, as well as how our relationships with one another may be strengthened and weakened. As with most of the chapters in part 2, this chapter is a blend of conceptual and practical analyses, with suggestions for future research and scholarly activity as well as implications for practice. We begin with a brief consideration of the self.

The Self

Much of psychology considers the topic of the self to be especially important. We wonder who we are, struggle with "finding ourselves," and more. Behavioral approaches turn away from the idea that the self is the cause of one's behavior, and instead turn the focus toward the environment. Some behavior analysts have conceptualized what it means to "know oneself." Skinner (1953, 1974), for example, focused on this when he considered the topic of self-knowledge and self-awareness. Here, self-knowledge is characterized as the extent to which one can describe their ongoing private events, predict their future behavior based on those events, and more (Hayes & Fryling, 2013). From our perspective, such self-knowledge pertains to detecting subtleties in one's public behavior.

Still, because it is the community that teaches us to talk about ourselves and to predict our behavior, we might say that self-knowledge is largely a reflection of our historical circumstances: Our self might be considered our personal and collective histories. And, to the extent that our histories entail events and circumstances that are not shared with others, each of us operates as a unique *self.* Of course, our histories are not entirely unique, nor are they entirely our own. Our histories overlap with those of others and the extent to which they do facilitates important behavior (e.g., altruistic acts). We build upon this foundation in the following sections, addressing perspective-taking and relationships with others. Elaborating upon our previous work in this area (DeBernardis et al., 2014), we turn now to the topic of perspective-taking.

Perspective-Taking

Perspective-taking may be defined in various ways, but generally refers to the behavior of taking another person's view, standing in their shoes or experiencing the world as another person would. This sort of behavior has obvious implications for one's interactions with others, including coworkers, friends, even strangers, as when one assumes that someone cutting you off on the freeway just didn't see you or was distracted by something else. As such, it isn't surprising that perspective-taking deficits tend to be associated with psychological distress (e.g., Vilardaga et al., 2012; Wolkenstein et al., 2011). The importance of understanding perspective-taking is further underscored by the range of research that has been conducted on the topic. Perspective-taking is studied in the disciplines of psychology, education, and business, among others. Our analysis of perspective-taking relies upon a condition of shared history, which we describe in detail in the next section.

Shared History

Along with our colleague, we have proposed an interbehavioral conceptualization of perspective-taking (DeBernardis et al., 2014). Our analysis of the topic builds upon the importance of interbehavioral history as a participant in all psychological happenings. In particular, perspective-taking focuses on a specific type of interbehavioral history, a **shared history** between the perceiver (the one taking the perspective of another) and the target (the one whom the perceiver is taking the perspective of). Of conceptual interest, there must also be an unshared history between the perceiver and the target in order for perspective-taking to occur. That is, if the perceiver and the target have roughly the same history in a particular situation, then there is no way for perspective-taking to occur, as the perceiver's perspective will be the same as the target's perspective. This is to say, the perceiver can't actually *be* the target, psychologically speaking. There must be some shared and some unshared history in a particular situation in order for perspective-taking to occur.

.

Duration. Further, the analysis we are making proposes that the shared interbehavioral history involved in perspective-taking can vary along the dimensions of both duration and quality. In this context, **duration** may be considered a quantitative measure of how long the perceiver and the target have had a shared history, whereas **quality** refers to the range of experiences involved in that shared history. All shared histories have some measure of duration and quality. For example, some shared histories have a long duration but are relatively narrow in scope as far as quality goes. Coworkers in a large organization may be good examples of such shared histories, particularly if they have worked together for an extended period of time. In this case, the perceiver may be good at taking the perspective of the target, but only in particular situations. And, the longer you work with someone, the better you may become at predicting the target's behavior in those situations.

Still, the perceiver's perspective-taking ability may remain relatively limited to the extent that the quality of the shared history is not extensive. For example, the perceiver might predict how the target will behave in a conflict situation with management but be uncertain as to how they might behave in nonwork settings. Similar assumptions might be made for one's extended family members. It's possible that a shared history permits one to predict how a relative might behave during a holiday gathering, but not how they would behave in a social setting where family members are not present.

Relationships of various sorts are also good examples of perspective-taking as a function of the duration of shared history. For example, one might think they know a friend or romantic partner fairly well, only to realize that this is not the case over time. Because a sense of knowing the other person has developed over the course of a shared history of some duration, we may be surprised when that person behaves in an unpredicted way. Knowing another by virtue of a shared history, even of long duration, is limited by the quality of that history and the fact that it evolves over time.

Quality. The above examples all pertained to situations where the duration of the shared history may have been long, perhaps resulting in a relatively strong perspective-taking ability on behalf of the perceiver, though limited to particular situations because the shared relationship lacked quality (in the sense of how we are using that term in this chapter). The opposite may happen, too. A perceiver could develop a shared history with someone that is of high quality, involving a wide range of experiences, in different settings, doing very different things, and so on. Perhaps the perceiver developed a friendship with someone (the target) and they quickly started doing almost everything together. Here the perceiver may predict the target's behavior to some extent, but this may be limited by the lack of duration involved in the shared history. That is, the perspective-taking ability of the perceiver may be deficient as a result of the short duration. Similar to the above example, this sort of shared history may also result in a situation where someone feels like they know someone very well (i.e., can engage in high levels of perspective-taking) because of the high quality of the shared history between them, but where they are surprised to learn that they actually don't know the target that well as their shared history increases in duration. To reiterate, from our interbehavioral perspective, all perspective-taking involves some shared history that varies along the dimensions of both quantity and quality.

Perspective-Taking Continuum

Elaborating upon the shared history involved in perspective-taking, DeBernardis et al. (2014) also proposed a continuum of perspective-taking behavior, in an attempt to capture the complexity involved in different instances of perspective-taking. The continuum involves five levels, as described below.

1) Absence. At one end of the perspective-taking continuum is the absence of perspective-taking. At this level there is no prediction of how another person would behave differently from how the perceiver is behaving. As noted by developmental psychologists, young children demonstrate this level of perspective-taking when they act as though their own perspective is the only perspective (e.g., Piaget & Inhelder, 1972). There is no recognition that another perspective is present in the situation. It also seems likely that a complete absence of perspective-taking is associated with some developmental disorders and severe psychopathology, resulting in limited development of social skills and interpersonal relationships.

.

2) Common Perspective-Taking. In common perspective-taking, there is some perspective-taking but it isn't dependent upon any particular shared history. That is, without any shared history at all, any perceiver would be able to predict the behavior of the target in common perspective-taking. As noted by DeBernardis et al. (2014), it is interesting that some of the popular perspective-taking measures in the research literature involve common perspective-taking. For instance, the common "Sally Anne" task that, among other things, involves a child (the perceiver) observing a marble being moved to a different location, knowing that the doll in question (the target) did not see that the marble was moved, would anticipate that the target would look for the marble in the initial location (e.g., Baron-Cohen et al., 1985). Again, this is not dependent on any particular shared history; anyone would respond to the task in this way. Though it is possible that perspective-taking deficits may still be found at this level, they are relatively basic perspective-taking deficits.

Similarly, the popular perspective-taking tasks studied within relational frame theory (e.g., McHugh et al., 2004; Montoya-Rodríguez et al., 2017), the deictic frames, are also not dependent on any particular shared history. These protocols, which assess the establishment of relational frames with respect to I-YOU, HERE-THERE, and NOW-THEN deictic cues do not depend upon a specific shared history. Indeed, it is expected that all participants in these studies would respond in the same way in order to demonstrate perspective-taking. In keeping with our comments above, it is noteworthy that these protocols have been found to be associated with various developmental disorders and psychopathology. Importantly, research has also shown that individuals can improve their perspective-taking ability through experiences with multiple-exemplar instruction with respect to the deictic frames targeted from a relational frame theory perspective (Hayes et al., 2001).

.

3) Conventional Perspective-Taking. Conventional perspective-taking is more complex than common perspective-taking in that it does involve some shared history. This level of perspective-taking behavior is referred to as "conventional" because it is not a unique shared history between the perceiver and target but is instead based on shared cultural conditions

(Kantor, 1982). We might predict that someone dressed very nicely takes care to manage how people perceive them, whereas someone who doesn't dress as nicely is less worried about how people view them. Various predictions can also be made based on a person's gender, religion, and other features that are considered to be cultural in nature. It may be important to note here that cultural conventions are always evolving, and this may influence perspective-taking accuracy in any particular instance. Here there is some shared history, but it is not the common perspective-taking of the previous level. Still, the shared history is not unique to the perceiver and target, as it pertains to a broader history shared among members of particular cultural collectivities.

4) Interpersonal Perspective-Taking. Interpersonal perspective-taking is more complex than conventional perspective-taking in that it involves a unique shared history between the perceiver and the target. In interpersonal perspective-taking, the shared history is unique to particular situations or settings. For example, if someone always observes a colleague complain about being overworked whenever a task is presented to them, they may predict that the colleague will again complain about being overworked when another task is presented to them. Similarly, one may have a friend who complains that their girlfriend doesn't give them enough attention when they are in public social circumstances. You may then predict that your friend would complain that their girlfriend didn't give them enough attention at a recent holiday gathering as well. Here the perspective-taking is considered interpersonal because it does depend on a unique, shared relationship between the perceiver and the target. Still, the perspective-taking may be somewhat limited in that it is based on particular situations or settings, and facilitates perspective-taking only with respect to those situations or settings.

5) Predictive Perspective-Taking. The final, most complex form of perspective-taking is predictive perspective-taking. While all perspective-taking involves making predictions about the target's behavior, this fifth and final level of perspective-taking involves making predictions about the target's behavior in novel situations. This sort of perspective-taking also involves a unique, shared history between the perceiver and the target. However, in this case, the perceiver is not only predicting what the target will do in a similar situation, as in interpersonal perspective-taking, but what they would do in a novel situation as well. This involves the perceiver responding to aspects of the shared history that are present in the novel situation, and then engaging in perspective-taking with respect to them. It is possible to view this as similar to the behavioral process of generalization, but here the perspective-taking is not based on physical similarity between the previous and the present situation. Rather, there is a similarity in the relationships among the factors present in the current situation and those of the shared history, such that an inference may be made by the perceiver. In fact, this sort of perspective-taking is more complex than interpersonal perspective-taking because it cannot be said to be a matter of generalization processes, which could be said of the latter.

While we suspect that perspective-taking evolves along the progression outlined in the continuum above, our primary aim is not to suggest a behavioral-developmental sequence of perspective-taking. Rather, our aim is to present different levels of complexity involved in perspective-taking to facilitate further study of this phenomenon. In our view, much of the current research on perspective-taking is focused on what we have called common perspective-taking, and it is possible that research may be further developed by considering the continuum described above.

There is one other matter that we would like to address with respect to the perspective-taking continuum, and that pertains to the involvement of language in perspective-taking ability.

Language and perspective-taking. Our consideration of perspective-taking requires us to discuss the role of language in perspective-taking repertoires. There is a long-standing debate regarding the extent to which individuals without language (including nonhuman animals) may engage in perspective-taking behavior (e.g., Novak, 2012). While an exploration of this is far beyond the scope of the present chapter, it is clear that language does participate in perspective-taking. Consider the example of predictive perspective-taking that we have just described. This particular level of perspective-taking involves predicting another person's behavior at some point *in the future*. Recall from previous chapters that the past and future involve time, and are constructs rather than events. Both the past and the future exist only in the present moment (Hayes, 1992b).

While the past and future are similar in this way, they also have distinctive features. In particular, while the past as the past can only exist as a present construct, there was a past that was previously present. As such, the past may participate in the present in the absence of language. By contrast, the future, which also only exists as a construct that can only occur in the present moment, never was. Put differently, while the past was previously present, the future only ever exists as a construct. Given this, predicting what someone may or may not do in the future necessarily involves language. The literature on relational frame theory and perspective-taking (e.g., Montoya-Rodríguez et al., 2017), with a focus on deictic relational framing, also seems to involve language, as there is some description of the target individual's behavior as distinct from someone else's. All of this requires that there is some linguistic action participating in perspective-taking. Importantly, this is not to say that language causes perspective-taking, but rather to acknowledge that perspective-taking, at least many forms of it, involves language.

As we have now considered perspective-taking, we turn to a closely related topic, interpersonal relationships.

Interpersonal Relationships

Relationships are central features of our lives. We have all sorts of relationships; we have relationships with friends, partners, coworkers, neighbors, people we interact with regularly at the local grocery store, and more. The fact that relationships are so prevalent in our lives may have something to do with us as a species. Indeed, scholars have suggested that increasing cooperation and connection were essential to the biological evolution of the human species (e.g., Atkins et al., 2019; Hayes & Sanford, 2014). The prevalence of relationships in the lives of human beings makes the topic worthy of consideration by researchers and clinicians working to understand human behavior. It comes as no surprise that the topic has been the focus of much research and clinical training already (e.g., Holman et al., 2017; Kanter et al., 2020).

While the literature on relationships is extensive and across various fields (e.g., workplace, romantic, and family relationships), one theme stands out, and it is pertinent to our aims in this chapter. Among all of the things studied in the area of relationships, consistent evidence points to the importance of relationship quality. That is, the sheer presence or absence of relationships is one thing; another thing is the importance of the quality of those relationships when they do exist. Research shows that relationship quality is associated with myriad health-related factors (e.g., Hooker et al., 2015). It makes sense that marital relationships have been the subject of much attention by researchers, and here too research points to the importance of relationship quality (Robles, 2014).

In earlier chapters we described how substitute stimulus functions develop and evolve. The present chapter builds upon this foundation and, in particular, emphasizes an important aspect of the development of substitute stimulus functions. Recall that substitute stimulus functions develop, for a given individual, under various conditions of spatiotemporal association, including stimuli and stimuli, stimuli and settings, stimuli and responding, and so on.

However, these association conditions, while necessary, are not sufficient for the development of substitute stimulus functions. Rather, an individual must respond with respect to those conditions for substitute stimulation to develop. In more common terms, we might say that an individual must notice, observe, or otherwise interact with the factors associated in the environment. In Kantor's (1924, p.323) words, "No connection between objects constitutes a fact for psychology unless such a connection operates to effect some form of reaction in an organism, still that connection need not be known by the organism to be actually functioning." This is to say, while stimuli may occur together in space and time, unless you respond with respect to those conditions, even if very subtly, subsequent substitution of the functions of each with those of the other may not occur. Understanding how there may be both closeness and conflict within interpersonal relationships is related to this issue. In the following section, we build upon our previous work describing how both closeness and conflict may be made more likely (Fryling & Hayes, 2019).

Closeness

We have suggested that the development of closeness in a relationship depends on the development of substitute stimulus functions by way of the aforementioned processes, responding with respect to association conditions (Fryling & Hayes, 2019). Most relationships involve two or more individuals being in relatively close spatiotemporal proximity to one another. This is to say they are being together. For example, they may spend time together talking on the phone, going places together, engaging in recreational activities together, and so on. Even reading a letter from a partner involves being together, as the letter serves as a substitute stimulus for the partner. Being together is a requirement for relationships to develop.

What happens during those association conditions is another thing, and this pertains to responding with respect as a requirement for substitute stimulation to develop. Spatiotemporal proximity alone isn't enough. Consider an instance of talking on the phone with a friend. Your friend may tell you about things going on in their life and how those things are related to other things. All of this involves conditions of association. A particularly good listener on this call may *respond* with respect to these association conditions, repeating them back, asking questions about them, and so on. This may help promote closeness: Your friend may report feeling heard. However, pertinent to our understanding of becoming *close,* the real benefit of this sort of interaction is more likely to occur in the future. This is because substitute stimulus functions are likely to have developed and may operate in subsequent interactions. As a result of responding with respect to association conditions during initial conversations, you may respond with respect to substitute stimulus functions, which are likely to be the same substitute stimulus functions to which your friend is responding. When this happens, your friend may feel a closer connection with you.

Of course, friendships develop over the course of many such conversations and other experiences. As these association conditions become more and more elaborate, along with our responding with respect to them, both of the friends may begin to feel closer to one another. This sort of process may explain why friends who have known each other for a long time sometimes report that they can pick up right where they left off even if they haven't talked in a while. Similarly, such closeness is evident when one reports that a friend "knows what I'm thinking about before even I do myself." (This topic also pertains to chapter 7 on inapparent events.)

Of course, these processes don't apply only to friendships. Similar examples could be described in the workplace, where coworkers who respond with respect to association conditions involving other coworkers are more likely to respond with respect to the same substitute stimulus functions as their coworkers. In these situations, they may be more likely to cooperate with one another. And, of course, this analysis applies to romantic relationships as well. Indeed, couples who respond with respect to association conditions involving their partners may increasingly respond with respect to the same substitute stimulations as their partners do.

Conflict

The above analysis of closeness in relationships also has implications for understanding conflict. As we have described, *responding with respect* to association conditions involving another person is key to developing closeness. By contrast, a failure to respond with respect to association conditions involving another person may contribute to conflict and prevent the development of substitute stimulus functions for the observer. Accordingly, the observer's responding will be less coordinated with that of the partner. Like the friendship example above, imagine that your friend Brenda told you that one of their friends, Tom, said something incredibly rude about her partner. Later, in another conversation, Brenda may mention crossing paths with Tom and how this made her feel uncomfortable. If you hadn't responded with respect to the initial association conditions (i.e., listened, psychologically speaking), then you might ask Brenda why she felt uncomfortable. This may create tension, not only in the moment, but a pattern of this sort could lead you and Brenda to feel distant from one another and could result in conflict. Similar to relationship closeness, relationship conflict can develop wherever relationships are occurring. This includes family members, coworkers, and partners in romantic relationships.

In summary, interbehavioral psychology gives us a unique way to conceptualize relationship closeness and conflict from a natural science perspective. Our analysis requires no pleas to hypothetical minds, inner feelings, or the private events that behaviorists are accustomed to speaking about (chapter 7). At the most basic level, the analysis points to the importance of having a shared history with another person as the foundation of a relationship. In order to develop a close relationship with someone, you must be exposed to association conditions involving them. An absence of this shared experience may explain why some couples stop spending time together or why friendships drift apart. But just being around another person isn't enough for the development of close relationships. A couple may drift apart while sitting on the same couch, for example. Indeed, it is the responding with respect to association conditions involving another person that is necessary for the development of shared substitute stimulation and essential to relationship closeness.

While this analysis is conceptually interesting, it also has practical implications. Relationship problems are multitudinous, and the benefits of healthy relationships are well researched and understood. Given this, it is important to consider factors that may promote relationship closeness and prevent conflict.

Applied Implications

Most analyses of relationship closeness and conflict appeal to explanatory notions of alleged inner happenings, particularly thoughts and feelings. Given this assumption, the only way one person might come to know what another person is thinking or feeling would be for the latter to tell the former. As such, communication may become the focus of research and practice in the analysis of relationships (see Kanter et al., 2020, for a recent review of common communication frameworks within this area of research). The idea here is that relationships could be improved if only the people involved communicated their thoughts and feelings more effectively.

From our perspective, while communication is necessary, it is not sufficient for the development of close relationships. The key to developing relationship closeness is the *responding with respect* to association conditions that occur while two people are communicating. This responding with respect shares some similarities with what is referred to in the literature as mindfulness. People's lives involve many association conditions, and it is likely that an individual may respond with respect to only a select number of these in any given situation. Mindfulness involves the deliberate focus on association conditions; to put it another way, mindfulness involves attending. In the context of relationships, mindfulness may encourage people to not only spend time together, but also to be "present" while they are doing so. This "being present" likely involves responding with respect to association conditions involving another person (including the communication mentioned above).

We have used to the term "mindfulness" here because of its presence in contemporary literature. However, we find the term to be distracting and vague because the specific reference to the mind, a hypothetical construct, may make mindfulness seem to be something internal, something that happens within. Obviously, things are always happening within biological organisms, but referring to all of this as mindfulness fails to point to the psychological processes involved or specifically what to do to improve things in any particular situation. Moreover, referring to such inner happenings, even if metaphorical, obstructs both research and practice.

Finally, we want to call attention to the implications of our analysis for understanding situations where someone may not want to have a close relationship with someone else. There are times when someone may prefer to have a relationship that is more distant. This could be the case when someone has many secrets that they prefer to keep private, where such secrets would be discovered by way of a shared history. Similarly, someone may find the closeness involved in relationships to be burdensome, such as when it interferes with work or some other task. These cases are mentioned because our analysis may also facilitate understanding unique situations where someone may actually prefer relationships that are not close, regardless of whether they are aware of this or not. Readers interested in this topic may also consider the topic of lying. Similar to keeping secrets, lying can occur only when a sufficiently shared history is absent (Fryling, 2016).

Summary and Key Points

This chapter addresses many topics pertaining to our relationships with ourselves and others. Included is an analysis of the self, the practice of perspective-taking, and the nature of interpersonal relationships. Perspective-taking was conceptualized as involving a shared history, and analyzed as a continuum based upon the duration and quality of that shared history. The topic of interpersonal relationships focused on how closeness and conflict may be promoted and inhibited, respectively, leading to a discussion of applied implications.

Study Questions

1. Describe the authors' conceptualization of the self.
2. How does a shared history pertain to the analysis of perspective-taking?
3. In what ways do both duration and quality of a shared history impact perspective-taking?
4. Why is it important to recognize that perspective-taking occurs along a continuum?
5. What benefits does the description of a continuum offer?
6. What factors contribute to both relationship closeness and conflict in the authors' view?

CHAPTER 10

Feelings

In this chapter we turn to the topic of feelings. Few would disagree with the observation that feelings are relevant to the understanding of many, if not most, psychological happenings. This is to say, feelings are pervasive and participate in much of our day-to-day lives. It's not just that feelings are pervasive in daily life that makes them worthy of specific consideration, though. Feelings also have unique features relative to other psychological events, and this uniqueness gives us even more reason to consider feeling events specifically. Kantor wrote about feelings in several places (e.g., Kantor 1926; Kantor & Smith, 1975), and we provide an overview and elaboration upon his analysis in this chapter. As we have done previously (Hayes & Fryling, 2017), we begin by differentiating the interbehavioral interpretation of feelings from other conceptualizations of such events, particularly those derived from behavior analytic foundations.

Common Perspectives on Feelings

Feelings have been conceptualized in many ways throughout both mainstream psychology and behavior analytic thinking. Most theories in traditional psychology place heavy emphasis on feelings as the causes of behavior. For example, aggression may be said to be caused by the feeling of anger, laughter by the feeling of joy or happiness, and so on. Based on this logic, controlling one's feelings is fundamental to changing one's behavior. The notion that feelings are causes of behavior is rejected in radical behavioral conceptualizations of feelings. Instead, feelings are held to be by-products of contingencies of reinforcement or punishment for **operant behavior** (Skinner, 1974). That is, we might feel happy or confident as a result of exposure to contingencies of positive reinforcement, and frustrated, depressed, or angry when exposed to conditions of extinction or punishment. Further, from a radical behavioral perspective, feelings are not just held to be by-products of operant contingencies; they are also considered to be private events. This is to say, inasmuch as feelings are held to be occurring inside the skin of the behaving organism, they are deemed observable only to the individual in whom they are occurring (e.g., Skinner, 1953, 1974). This feature distinguishes private feeling events from behaviors of the public sort in important ways. As mentioned in chapter 7, while interpreting these happenings as private by-products of contingencies eliminates the problem of conceptualizing feelings as hypothetical causal agents, there are a number of other problematic issues to consider. We provide an overview of some of these problems below. And, as we have done elsewhere (Hayes & Fryling, 2017), we distinguish between conceptual and practical problems.

Conceptual Issues

Our first conceptual concern with the analysis of feelings as private events pertains to the problem of reductionism (see Kantor, 1953). If feelings are held to be happening within the skin of the behaving individual, they may then be interpreted as visceral reactions. While being interested in the visceral reactions involved in feeling events is not problematic in and of itself, an analysis of the visceral reactions involved in feeling events is not a psychological analysis of feelings. Importantly, biological and psychological analyses are valid in their own right. However, problems arise when one is confused with the other or when one is reduced to the other on the grounds that the latter is considered to be more basic. The tendency to confuse biological and psychological subject matters is especially likely given the prevalence of what Kantor refers to as the "basis fallacy" throughout science and society more generally (Observer, 1969). Evidence of operating upon this fallacy is present in the radical behavioral interpretation of feelings because it encourages an understanding of psychological events by way of a study of "more basic" biological happenings.

A second problem with the radical behavioral interpretation of feeling events is that it overlooks the relational nature of psychological events. As we have emphasized in earlier chapters, the focus of a psychological event is a function obtaining between stimulating and responding. As such, responding cannot be understood in the absence of stimulating, and vice versa. When feelings are held to be events of a private sort, happening within the individual, analyses are aimed at achieving a more thorough understanding of the biological participants involved in such events—particularly those of the neurological type. Again, while this subject matter is certainly worthy of study, its study does not contribute to an understanding of feelings as psychological events.

Related to our concerns pertaining to the relational character of psychological events is the neglect of the environmental participants in feelings. One of the most fundamental aims of all behavioral positions is to shift the focus away from the person and toward the environmental context. This shift in focus has served to undermine the notion that the person is the agent of their own action. The radical behavioral view of feelings as private events overlooks the environmental participants in those events and, in doing so, retreats from one of the overarching aims of behavioral psychology.

Finally, as we have argued in chapter 3, psychological events involve the responding of the whole organism (Kantor, 1958). Focusing on the actions of the whole organism prevents interpretations of psychological events as actions of its organismic parts and sustains the distinction between biological and psychological happenings.

In summary, both the traditional and the radical behavioral conceptualizations of feelings present hurdles that prevent the development of a distinctly psychological analysis of feelings from a natural science perspective.

Practical Problems

We have just outlined the conceptual problems related to the analysis of feelings. Of course, conceptual issues are rarely unrelated to practical problems, and the analysis of feelings is no exception. For one, the inaccessibility of feelings as conceptualized as private events renders them something that can't be studied. Radical behaviorists may be quick to respond to this by suggesting that someone might study their own private events. Still, the inaccessibility of feeling events to external observers presents a problem for researchers and practitioners. Both are interested in the analysis of complex human behavior, in which feelings are surely involved. We cannot move forward with the study of feelings in behavior science if our most widely embraced conceptual analyses of these happenings prevent it.

A second issue pertains to how one comes to learn about themselves or develop what Skinner (1957, 1974) referred to as self-knowledge. According to Skinner, self-knowledge, like knowledge in general, is acquired under the auspices of a verbal community, which is to say the verbal community teaches us to talk about ourselves. However, inasmuch as the verbal community doesn't have access to the learner's private events, including feelings, the extent to which the verbal community can facilitate the development of self-knowledge with regard to one's feelings is limited. This is why behavior analysts encourage reliance on public happenings for the development of self-knowledge, including plausible public accompaniments and collateral public responses (e.g., Skinner, 1957, 1974). Thus, the conceptualization of feelings as private events impacts the practical issue of developing self-knowledge with respect to one's feelings (Hayes & Fryling, 2013).

Finally, the interpretation of feelings as events of the private class suggests that we may have to rely on the physiologist of the future to explain events of this sort. Although it is surely the case that instrumentation and techniques related to the analysis of internal, biological happenings have improved over time, those improvements still fail to bring us closer to an analysis of feelings as psychological events.

Now that we have described some of the conceptual and practical concerns related to the radical behavioral analysis of feelings, we turn to the interbehavioral perspective on this topic. Before moving on, we want to emphasize that the above-mentioned concerns with the analysis of feelings as private events are less about critiquing radical behaviorism and more about describing an alternative more susceptible to investigation.

Feelings from an Interbehavioral Perspective

As mentioned at the beginning of the chapter, feelings are important to consider not only because they are so much a part of our day-to-day lives, but also because they have several unique features relative to psychological events more generally. We turn now to these features and Kantor's analysis of feeling events. We begin by reviewing the most distinguishing feature of feeling events, namely their affective character. The affective character of feeling events accounts for their pervasiveness, including their extension over time. Finally, we consider feeling events to be a type of cultural happening and describe their conventional nature in humans who engage in linguistic activities.

Feelings Are Affective Actions

First, and most fundamentally, feelings require us to distinguish between affective and effective actions. Feelings are affective actions. They differ from effective actions in the sense that affective actions don't result in a change in the stimuli to which they occur. Rather, feelings result in changes in the reaction systems of the individual. Put another way, effective actions change the environment in some way, whereas affective actions change the reaction systems of the individual in some way.

For example, when another driver attempts to cut us off in traffic, we might honk the horn, which, in turn, may have an impact on the other driver. This would be an effective action in the sense that it brings about a change in the stimulating environment. By contrast, we may also feel afraid or angry upon being cut off. The feeling action doesn't change the stimulating environment in the same way as an effective action does. Rather, it changes the reaction systems of the behaving individual. For example, our muscles may become tense and our heart rate may be elevated. These changes in our reaction systems may be accompanied by changes in other actions, including those of an effective type. The dynamic and topographical properties of our speech may change, for example. The point is that feelings don't effect changes in the environment directly.

Similarly, we may ask a friend for a hug after not seeing them for a long time. This request may be considered an effective action in the sense that it results in the friend giving us a hug. This is contrasted with the feeling of happiness or closeness with the friend, which is affective and changes our reaction systems. Importantly, while we are indeed referring to some visceral happenings here, we are not suggesting that feelings are these visceral happenings. This is an important issue for us to be extra clear on, as suggesting that feelings are glandular activities would be confusing feeling actions with their effects on the biological conditions of the individual (Hayes & Fryling, 2017). This affective character of feeling events is by far the most distinguishing and significant feature of feelings.

Feelings Are Pervasive

The affective character of feeling events has several implications. In this section, we focus on how the affective character of feelings relates to feelings being pervasive. The fact that feeling events do not change the environment but rather the reaction systems of the individual means that things that stimulate feeling actions could also stimulate effective actions at the same time. Put differently, affective actions don't interfere with effective actions. Consistent with our previous example, we may interact with being cut off in traffic by both honking the horn and feeling afraid, and these two actions can happen simultaneously. Similarly, you can turn on your car while feeling upset, iron your clothes while feeling joyful, and so on. The same could not be said of two effective actions. For example, a person cannot open a door and shut the door, throw a ball and catch a ball, or iron their clothes and fold their clothes at the same time. Only one effective action may be made with respect to a particular stimulus at a time. Affective and effective actions can co-occur, such as when you talk to someone about politics (effective action) while also feeling angry (affective action). Affective and effective actions do not "compete" in the same way that two effective actions do.

Similarly, feelings may also occur independently of other sorts of action. Consistent with the previous example, a feeling action may occur with respect to a particular topic of conversation at dinner, and that feeling action may also occur while you drive home from dinner. In other words, feelings are not tied to specific effective actions. Rather, a multitude of responses and contexts may be associated with a particular affective action. All of this underscores the fact that feeling events are unique in the sense that they can occur at any time and in any place. This is why we say that feelings are pervasive.

The implicit functioning of feeling actions makes them even more pervasive. We may feel angry while having a conversation with someone at dinner (as in the previous example), and in the future feel angry when that person's name is mentioned, or while eating at the restaurant where the conversation occurred, and so on. This is to say, we may engage in feeling actions with respect to stimulating circumstances that have been previously associated with the original stimulus conditions. Feelings may constitute implicit responses with respect to substitute stimulation.

The properties of feelings thus far described means that feelings are occurring with respect to a wide range of original and substitutive circumstances. That is, association conditions may become very elaborate, with feeling actions becoming more and more disconnected from the circumstances under which they initially occurred. Someone may feel angry or sad at a given moment, such that a companion may ask them why they are so upset. How they answer that question is another matter (e.g., they may be subject to the social context), but it is likely that the feeling is so complex, implicit, and historical that they don't even know why they are feeling as they do. This issue is related to the intensity of feeling actions as well. We may feel strongly about something when we interact with it directly, but as substitution networks become more and more elaborate, feelings may become less intense to the point that they are just a faint sense of discomfort. These issues remind us that feelings aren't just unique; they are also incredibly complex and multifactored.

Thus far we have focused on the affective character of feelings as well as their pervasive, implicit character. We now turn to feelings as uniquely extended events.

Feelings Are Extended Over Time

As affective actions that have their primary impact on the reaction systems of individuals, feelings do not have clear beginnings and endings. This may result in feelings being more extended and prolonged over time. We may feel angry for hours or even days, for example. Similarly, we may feel happy or be in a good mood for an extended duration. This feature makes it possible for feelings to become associated with many stimuli and conditions of association by which substitutional functions of stimuli may be acquired. Accordingly, we may feel afraid or worried about something for an extended period of time under a multitude of setting conditions. It's easy to imagine how a feeling may occur in the context of a decision at work, and then becomes associated with conversations over dinner at a restaurant, whereby the restaurant develops substitute stimulus functions, and so on.

There are many examples that draw attention to the extended nature of feeling events.

Interestingly, we may begin to manage which situations we expose ourselves to as a result of our experiencing the extended nature of feeling events. For example, someone may say they "can't watch the news late at night." Presumably this is because the news often contains stories that stimulate intense feelings that may persist over an extended period of time. By contrast, a familiar show, or one that is humorous, may be preferred for the same reason.

Feeling events may also participate as setting conditions, and the fact that feeling events may be extended over time contributes to their operation as such (Kantor, 1924). Recall that setting conditions are factors that participate in psychological events, and as all participants, any change in the factors comprising the setting results in a reconfiguration of the entire event. Engaging in work-related tasks while also feeling happy is entirely different than engaging in work-related tasks while also feeling angry, for example. In this case, it is important to avoid confusing psychological events with their participation as setting factors for other psychological events (see Hayes & Fryling, 2014).

Feelings Are Cultural Happenings

Lastly, feeling events are cultural happenings (more on this in chapters 6 and 11). This feature of feeling events gives us an opportunity to reemphasize an important aspect of the interbehavioral analysis of feelings. That is, although biological factors participate in feeling events, those factors are not feeling events themselves. For the most part, feeling events are cultural in type (Kantor, 1982; Hayes & Fryling, 2009b). From an interbehavioral perspective, cultural events involve stimulus functions that have become institutionalized such that particular people respond similarly with respect to them, thereby becoming members of a specific collectivity. Feelings vary in accordance with the practices of a group and for this reason are cultural in type. Certain feelings, including happiness, anger, and fear, may be alike within groups and different across them—a circumstance that may be attributed to linguistic practices within groups. Kantor and Smith (1975, p.228) state, "We may be culturalized to love and hate things and persons which call out opposite responses in individuals from other families or national groups. Objects that arouse anger and fear in the members of one community may simply not do so for members of other groups or may stimulate quite other responses."

Cultural behavior, then, occurs with respect to attributed as opposed to natural properties of stimuli. The attribution of properties to stimuli is accomplished by linguistic activity, which is itself cultural in type. As nonhuman organisms don't engage in linguistic activity, they are not able to attribute properties to stimuli, nor are they able to react to properties of these sorts.

Accordingly, the feeling actions of nonhumans are coordinated only with the natural properties of stimulus objects. As such, they are not as complex or as differentiated as the feeling actions of humans. By contrast, human feelings evolve, becoming increasingly elaborate and increasingly coordinated with substitute stimulation.

Summary and Key Points

Our primary aim in this chapter was to outline the unique features of feeling events from an interbehavioral perspective. We began with a review of common approaches to the topic of feelings in both psychology and behavior analysis. We then highlighted both conceptual and practical concerns related to these analyses, so as to point to the need for an alternative approach. From an interbehavioral perspective, feelings are affective actions, and most of their distinctive features follow from this characteristic. Given their affective character, feelings are pervasive, implicit, and extended over time. Further, we made the point that feelings are complicated by linguistic activity in a cultural context.

Study Questions

1. What is the common or traditional perspective on the role of feelings in the analysis of behavior? Why are these views of

feelings inconsistent with the perspective in this text?

2. Explain the practical problems related to the analysis of feelings as private events.

3. Distinguish between affective and effective actions and explain why this is fundamental to the interbehavioral analysis of feeling events.

4. Feeling events have several unique characteristics, as outlined in this chapter. Provide an example that highlights how feelings are pervasive and extended over time.

5. How does the conceptualization of feelings as cultural happenings further help distinguish a psychological analysis of feelings from a biological analysis of feelings?

CHAPTER 11

Human Development

This chapter considers the topic of human development from an interbehavioral perspective. As with many topics considered throughout this book, the interbehavioral analysis of psychological development is closely involved with the interbehavioral field construction (e.g., Hayes & Fryling, 2018; Kantor, 1958; chapter 3 of this book). Among other things, this construction recognizes that interbehavioral history participates in all ongoing psychological events. Actually, from an interbehavioral perspective, the presence of history in our psychological interactions is one thing that distinguishes psychological events from the events of other sciences (e.g., biology or physics; Fryling & Hayes, 2009).

As you may imagine, the presence of interbehavioral history is of particular relevance to our analysis of psychological development, the focus of the present chapter. Specifically, in this chapter we elaborate upon the concept of interbehavioral history and focus on factors that influence or participate in its development, as described by Kantor and Smith (1975, pp.59–73). We then provide some comments on the behavior analytic understanding of development and outline how behavior analytic researchers may begin to study it more specifically. To conclude the chapter, we consider the topic of aging from an interbehavioral perspective.

Interbehavioral History

An individual's interbehavioral history begins early, as soon as interactions with the stimulating environment begin (i.e., even before birth). With that said, Kantor and Smith (1975) note that an individual's psychological life largely begins at birth. One's history of psychological interactions corresponds closely with biological maturation, particularly during early childhood. Simply put, greater levels of biological development allow for a greater range of contacts with the stimulating environment. A child encounters a "larger" environment once they are able to grasp objects and stand, even more so when they begin to walk, talk, and so on. These obvious examples show how closely biological and psychological development correspond to one another, particularly during early childhood.

At the same time, there are many differences between biological and psychological development. For one, as biological organisms, humans mature up to age twenty-five to thirty years, after which they begin to decline. That is, humans do not continue to develop more and more expansive biological systems. Rather, our biological systems reach a point of being more or less fully developed, and from there on begin a process of gradual deterioration. By contrast, there is no point at which one's psychological development ceases. (We will comment on psychological decline when we consider aging later in this chapter, though.) As soon as someone begins to develop psychologically, they continue to do so until the end of life. One's psychological history just becomes more and more elaborate.

This key distinction between biological and psychological development is worth reiterating before we move on. While biological development and psychological development *influence* one another, and we will elaborate on this a bit below, psychological development is unique in that it keeps going throughout one's lifetime. The same cannot be said for physical or biological development.

Kantor and Smith (1975, pp.62–65) remind us of two fundamental interbehavioral principles related to the distinction between psychological and biological development:

1. Psychological reactions are not mere functions of biological structures.
2. Biological factors *participate* in psychological behavior.

These two principles remind us that psychological happenings are not a result of, or caused by, biological structures. At the same time, while biological structures are not the cause of psychological happenings, biological factors do indeed participate in or are necessary for various psychological actions to occur. We elaborate on both biological and cultural factors influencing interbehavioral history below.

Factors Influencing Interbehavioral History

Given the importance of interbehavioral history in the analysis of human development, we turn now to both biological and cultural factors that influence how interbehavioral history unfolds over the course of one's lifetime.

•

Biological Influences. At a very general level, the interbehavioral history of any individual member of a species is influenced by the biological evolution of the species to which they belong. The interbehavioral histories of humans, for example, are influenced by the organization of our organs, the physical structures of our bodies, and so on. Right away it's important to clarify that this only makes it possible for certain types of psychological development to occur. Just because someone is a member of a species that walks and talks doesn't mean that they will necessarily walk and talk themselves, for example. Similarly, while we know that certain "milestones" are likely to occur at various times during childhood development, that around X months a child will likely be able to crawl, stand, take steps with assistance, walk, and more, these are not automatic or assured. A particular psychological history is required. As Kantor and Smith (1975, p.66) state, "This is the only legitimate sense in which we may speak of a biological basis for psychological phenomena."

Along these lines we can imagine that interbehavioral history is also greatly influenced by individual differences in biological development. A variety of individual differences (e.g., neurodiversity, medical conditions, etc.) impact how any particular member of a species develops. Depending on the specifics of these individual differences, there may be more or less of an influence on one's interbehavioral history.

Cultural Influences. The cultural context also participates in how interbehavioral history develops. Different group circumstances result in different contacts with the environment, presenting different opportunities for repertoires or skills to evolve, and this has a significant impact on what may or may not ultimately develop. In an obvious example, we know that individuals don't just learn to talk, they learn to talk in a particular language, and in a particular way even within languages. Moreover, people think about things in particular ways, develop attitudes, and more, all of which occurs within a cultural context. In Kantor and Smith's words

(1975, p.68), "The psychological possibilities contributed by cultural conditions are supplied mainly by the opportunities for contacts with stimuli."

The influence of cultural factors on interbehavioral history is pervasive. If we were to think of many of the things we are good at, not good at, know nothing about, and more, we can probably identify cultural circumstances that set the stage for that interbehavioral history to be possible. Different groups of people become known for their taste in art, food, cooking abilities, religious beliefs, and so on. These influences are so great that they can be overlooked altogether, whereby some qualitative difference between people of different groups is assumed (Kantor & Smith, 1975).

Thus far, we have drawn attention to the role interbehavioral history plays in understanding human development. We have distinguished psychological development from that of other sciences, and highlighted how both biological and cultural factors participate in how psychological development unfolds over the course of one's lifetime.

We will now consider what behavior analytic research on development would look like given this perspective—and question whether studies that are sometimes considered to be developmental in type are properly focused on understanding psychological development.

Behavior Analysis and Development

We might start this section by asking a question: What does a study of psychological development from a behavior analytic perspective look like? To help answer this question, we should first consider how most applied research happens in behavior analysis. In general, experiments have a baseline and an intervention condition, and the extent to which an improvement/change in behavior has occurred as a result of some manipulation (i.e., intervention condition) is observed. We do this in several ways—through reversal designs, multiple-baseline designs, alternating treatment designs, and so on (Kazdin, 2011).

Largely, these research studies help us answer questions like "Does this intervention work?" or maybe "How well does this intervention work?" These are important questions to ask, as we are most interested in knowing which interventions are helpful and just how helpful they are. Obviously, we should use interventions that reliably result in meaningful behavior change. Some research designs allow for a comparison of different interventions to see which one works better or worse. Again, these are important research questions to ask.

While these studies produce meaningful information, it isn't clear that they tell us much about psychological development specifically. Research on psychological development requires going beyond these traditional questions, as it is focused not on whether or not a particular intervention works, but on sequences of events. That is, research in psychological development would study how one thing leads to another thing, and to another thing. For this reason, it isn't surprising that a lot of what we consider to be traditional developmental research involves longitudinal studies—we wouldn't know how one thing leads to another if we didn't study it *over time*. Development doesn't "work" or not work. Some of this research is happening in behavior analysis. For example, Greer and colleagues (e.g., Greer & Ross, 2008) have examined the extent to which teaching one skill leads to another skill being learned more quickly. The concept of behavioral cusps is related to this, as a behavioral cusp (Rosales-Ruiz & Baer, 1997) refers to a behavior change that results in the individual being exposed to new contingencies of reinforcement (i.e., if the individual learns to do this, then they'll be able to learn how to do that). However, there is no way to know whether something is a cusp unless sequences of behaviors are measured, including different behaviors at different times.

Understanding the need for research on psychological development to focus on sequences of happenings is one thing. Actually, conducting studies on these sequences is another. We imagine that studies on psychological development of the sort herein proposed would require more time and detailed planning than applied behavior analysts may be accustomed to conducting.

A science of psychology that includes an understanding of development requires us to head in this direction. And, we *need* a science that includes a significant focus on development. Indeed, it isn't all that helpful to simply know whether or not something produced a change. We also need to know what was present before that change (e.g., what occurred before such that the change was more or less likely), and then also how that change resulted in some other thing happening.

A developmental understanding is required for a comprehensive science, including a more fully informed, effective practice. Including studies with children as participants doesn't make a study developmental in nature. In fact, from a behavior analytic perspective, the age of the participant may not be of much interest at all (it could be of interest assuming some general biological influences mentioned above). Again, developmental research from a psychological perspective requires a focus on sequences of happenings. Moreover, given the influence of biology and cultural factors on interbehavioral history, the study of human development is ripe with opportunities for interdisciplinary collaboration, as we have discussed earlier in this text.

Biological and Psychological Decline with Advancing Age

We have talked about psychological development in a very general sense up to this point, focusing our discussion on the development of interbehavioral history in childhood. We now turn to a discussion of the psychological aspects of advancing age. In the material to follow we comment further on the distinction between the biological and psychological aspects of aging with the aim of acknowledging the impact of the former on the latter. We also provide an interbehavioral analysis of some telling examples of psychological deterioration in old age. We conclude with some remarks on the value of practices deemed helpful in staving off intellectual decline.

Before moving on to these issues, a comment on cultural practices designed to sustain one's social capital over the period of advancing age seems warranted. To sustain our value as productive members of society, we are inclined to present ourselves favorably, and what is most favorable in our society is youth. Indeed, youth is so highly valued in our culture that our members are induced to disguise their age as long as they possibly can, and oftentimes longer than convincing. Advancing age is evident in appearance, significant gains and losses of weight, varicose veins, hair loss and discoloration, wrinkles, crows' feet, brown spots, and yellow teeth. To disguise these conditions, we can have tummy tucks, hair dyes and replacements, face-lifts, Botox injections, wrinkle creams, spot removers, and miracle potions. And coupled with this, it is considered impolite to ask a person, especially a woman, their age. Accordingly, it is considered acceptable for a woman to lie about her age in our culture.

These are all practices aimed at disguising the biological indicators of aging. The psychological indicators of advancing age, specifically intellectual decline, are not as readily disguised. Sustaining our social capital in this domain is achieved, largely, by avoiding circumstances in which our decline might be noticed.

Biological Decline

As previously mentioned, biological development in human beings reaches maturity at approximately thirty years of age, after which is a period of gradual deterioration culminating in death. The changes observed in a person over the period of their decline are both biological and psychological. However, the pace and period of biological deterioration is more certain than is that of psychological decline. Indeed, as Kantor and Smith (1975) point out, long after an individual has entered a period of biological decline, their psychological growth may continue to expand. In their words, "There is no point at which the psychological growth of an organism necessarily ceases. Even during the deterioration period of old age, he can enter into new types of interactions with objects and continue to develop psychologically even to the very moment of death" (p.62).

Psychological Decline

Despite the divergence of the biological and psychological aspects of individuals' life histories, biological deterioration may have a deleterious impact on continued psychological development as mentioned above. As such, we may consider the psychological aspects of advancing age, at least to some extent, as secondary to its biological aspects.

Among the biological conditions impacted by aging are sensory capacities. Some of these capacities, namely seeing and hearing, are correctable to some degree with glasses and hearing aids. Seeing and hearing are not mere organismic happenings, though. Like all other types of psychological events, seeing and hearing are actions with respect to stimulation. This being the case, continued deterioration of biological structures eventuates in diminished or otherwise altered contact with stimulation, particularly stimulation inhering in the natural properties of environing things, including other people. Hence, in addition to being somewhat less able to navigate the physical environment with diminished sensory capacities of these sorts, it is likely that these disabilities will have a deleterious effect on social interactions as well.

Taste and smell are also impacted with advancing age. Taste buds lose their sensitivity and ability to regenerate, enhancing preference for sugar and salt over more subtle tastes. Olfactory nerve endings and mucus production in the nose may also decline, weakening the sense of smell. Neither of these two conditions is readily correctable. Fortunately, their losses, while no doubt eliminating the pleasures of delicious food and fragrant flowers, don't engender social isolation to the same extent as losses of vision and hearing do.

It is not just sensory capacities that decline with age. It is also organ systems, bones, and muscles. For example, aging individuals may come to experience shortness of breath, light-headedness, or fatigue—either alone or in conjunction with bodily conditions of other sorts, including organ system failures and diseases. Added to these, elders may have joint pain, develop arthritis or osteoporosis, or suffer failures of the hips and knees. Some of these problems may be corrected—again to some extent and at least for a while—with drugs, for example, or body part replacements, and so on.

Still, continued deterioration of these systems inhibits participation in social activities, including those of long-standing duration. No more golfing outings or tennis matches and, eventually, no more getting up from a fall, or climbing stairs, or walking. Thus, more than participating in treasured social activities is lost with a lack of mobility. More importantly, in this bodily state, elders are very likely to be confined to a particular location, such as a room or a set of rooms through which, with the help of others, they can move about. This has the effect of diminishing the stimuli available for interaction. To put it colloquially, when we don't get around much anymore, we live in a smaller world.

In addressing the impact of biological deterioration on continued psychological growth, we have focused on interactions with the functions of stimulus objects inhering in their natural properties and on opportunities to contact multitudinous stimulus objects. As we have described earlier in this text, psychological interactions with stimuli are not limited to the functions inhering in the natural properties of stimulus objects, and not being in the presence of particular stimulus objects does not prevent interactions with stimulation having their original sources in those objects. We turn, then, to the implications of these mitigating circumstances.

First, not all or even most of the stimulus functions of stimulus objects inhere in their natural properties. From a very early point in the psychological life of a human being, roughly coincident with the development of language, responding unrelated to the physical properties of stimulus objects begins to be acquired and quickly thereafter becomes the dominant type of psychological activity (Kantor, 1982, p.179.) In other words, responding is then coordinated with functions attributed to stimulus objects by way of linguistic activity. Our point in making this analysis is to draw attention to the fact that the decline of sensory capacities in advancing age may have a deleterious effect on psychological interactions with stimulation inherent in the natural properties of stimulus objects. Thus, avoiding a rock in one's path depends on one's ability to see the rock. However, not being able to see the rock does not prevent one from engaging in the conventional behavior of talking about it.

Second, we may address the observation that responding with respect to stimulation having its source in a particular stimulus object may occur in the absence of that object. As previously noted, sensory activities such as seeing and hearing are not just organismic happenings. They are also actions with respect to stimulating, and if the original source of the stimulus functions with which such actions are taking place are absent, then it must be assumed that those functions are operating from another presently available source. This is to say, the functions are substitutional.

The features of psychological events thus far described are further complicated by their historical nature, as described above. Specifically, an individual's psychological responses with respect to stimulus functions, be they inherent, conventional, or substitutional, depend on the individual's historical interactions with those stimuli.

Having characterized psychological events as to how they may be altered by biological decline, as well as the circumstances mitigating these outcomes to some extent, we may examine the process of decline in particular types of psychological activities. Specifically, we offer an interpretation of what may be happening when our thinking and remembering activities decline over the course of normal aging in two particular instances: losing words and diminished intellectual activity.

•

Losing Words. One circumstance familiar to persons of advancing age is what is referred to as "losing words." This is a circumstance in which previously performed verbal responses, under what appear to be typical stimulus conditions for their occurrence, fail to be emitted. Generally speaking, "losing words" is embarrassing, and one means of avoiding embarrassment is to shy away from circumstances in which this evidence of old age is likely to be noticed or, if stuck in such circumstances, to say very little. Neither of these solutions to the problem is helpful in the longer run, though, as the first assures even greater social isolation, and the latter confirms others' suspicions of one's decline—and with it, some portion of one's social capital.

Forgetting a name is a common example. Skinner (1983) commented on the circumstance of momentarily forgetting a name by saying that names "have so little going for them in terms of context" (1983, p.347). He does not elaborate. (Rather, he goes on to describe various ways to conceal the fact of having forgotten the name.) We agree that the loss of the name is a matter of contextual circumstances. We also feel that further elaboration as to what may be occurring under these circumstances is warranted.

To begin, we may acknowledge that a stimulus object may be a source of multiple stimulus functions, both original and substitutive, and which of this multitude of functions may be expected to operate in any given psychological event field is a matter of setting conditions. In other words, stimulus functions are actualized by setting conditions. Names as responses are peculiar to specific stimuli, and responses to highly specific stimuli occur under highly specific contextual circumstances. Not coming up with a person's name at a given moment means that the contextual circumstances under which a stimulus function coordinated with that name is not actualized. In short, the context is not specific enough to ensure the operation of this function. As such, if social circumstances were to permit, the name might become available by engaging in related actions through which the needed context could be concatenated.

.

Diminished Intellectual Activity. We may also consider the decline of intellectual activities with advancing age. Skinner talks about it becoming "harder to 'think big thoughts' in the sense of moving from one part of a paragraph to another or from one part of a chapter to another" (1983, p.152). In accounting for this failure, he says that the "intraverbal connections are weak, and inconsistencies are therefore likely" (p.152), but he doesn't offer an explanation as to why the intraverbal connections are weak or how they have become so. In short, no *analysis* of these sorts of psychological events is provided. We think an analysis of the process of intellectual decline in old age is worthy of consideration.

As previously described, a given object may be a source of multiple stimulus functions, and each of these functions bears relations with many others, such that the operation of one actualizes the operations of others depending on the setting in which they are occurring. Further, we may be reminded that the acquisition of stimulus functions throughout the psychological life of a person is continuous and that whatever functions are acquired are not lost or forgotten, but rather evolve in terms of becoming coordinated with ever more elaborate responses. Psychological events are historical in this sense. From this perspective, we may examine the impact of aging on the most complex of psychological events, namely those of the intellectual type.

Like all other types of psychological actions, intellectual activities are acquired over the course of a lifetime. They may be characterized, roughly, as extended patterns of interaction involving responses of arbitrary form coordinated with attributed properties of stimuli. The complications of thinking, planning, remembering, and other varieties of intellectual behavior we suggest are due to their involving stimulus functions many times removed from original sources, operating in long strings or networks.

Such activities are sustained in good order by their continued engagement under conditions explicitly designed to minimize their interruption and disruption. These are conditions in which ongoing interactions of a particular sort comprise setting conditions under which subsequent interactions of the same sort are actualized. In advancing age, the engagement in intellectual activities to the extent needed to create the context of setting for their preservation is not likely to be maintained, and with it goes the capacity for continued intellectual activity to a previous standard.

We suggest that two features of intellectual activity are especially vulnerable to advancing age. First, the more remote the connection of stimulus functions to original sources and the less specific the setting, the less likely a response is to be available. Second, the fact that intellectual activities occur as extended patterns of activity means that there is ample opportunity for their occurrences to be interrupted by more immediate concerns. Among these concerns may be physical conditions common to persons of advancing age, such as bodily discomfort, failing eyesight, fatigue, and so on (Skinner, 1983). Added to these are disruptions due to the actualization of irrelevant but nonetheless related stimulus functions. These are activities coordinated with stimulus functions not so far removed from their original sources, particularly those to which responses are more likely to be executed effectively. Circumstances of this sort are commonly referred to as a loss of "executive function"—which, unfortunately, implicates a biological circumstance of an unknown sort. In sum, a failure to execute intellectual action to a previously achieved standard sets the occasion for other behavior to take its place. It is not a failure to respond per se. It is just a circumstance of doing something else.

As we see it, for the reasons just discussed, complex intellectual behaviors are probably the first to deteriorate with advancing age. Fortunately for persons of advancing age, much of this sort of activity takes place when they are alone, wherein they are serving as both the speaker and the listener. Hence, whatever failures an old person experiences in attempting to execute intellectual activities are largely unknown to others. And, rather than produce an incoherent verbal product—either by voice or in writing—aging intellectuals just tend to stop engaging in intellectual behavior of the sort they once did. We understand that they have "retired."

In concluding this discussion of intellectual decline with advancing age, we may return to the matter of social capital. When people's worth in society is derived from estimations of their relative youth, it is understandable that they would find ways of disguising their advancing age. We have commented on strategies employed for this purpose, noting that different processes of decline tend to be disguised in different ways. Generally speaking, biological decline is disguised by fixing our appearance—by dyeing our hair, tending to our wrinkles, etc. By contrast, psychological decline is disguised by discontinuing our participation in social activities.

The discomforts of aging—both the deterioration of our capacities and our inability to hide it effectively—have given rise to a literature on how to stave off what can't be hidden, namely intellectual decline. Most of the practices advocated for this purpose have to do with keeping a particular part of the organism, namely the brain, active. Various exercises to keep the brain active have been devised. For the most part, these exercises are designed to maintain and build up connections among the various things going on in this organ. While connections among things are surely important to maintain, this strategy seems unnecessarily indirect. As we see it, the most important connections to be maintained are those between stimulus functions and setting factors. After all, it is these connections that brain exercises may help sustain. Thus, it might be better to focus on the historical interactions of the whole organism with its exceedingly complex environment than to focus on what may be happening in one of its organs.

Summary and Key Points

In this chapter we have examined the perpetual elaboration of interbehavioral history through the ongoing process of psychological development in the life circumstances of human beings. From this perspective, we suggested that behavior analytic studies aimed at observing and changing the behavior of children at a particular point in their development are not studies of development. Instead, we argued that understanding the process of psychological development requires longitudinal studies of event sequences, with a focus on how one event leads to another and another over time.

We also discussed the differences between the biological and psychological aspects of aging, making the case that psychological development continues long after biological maturity is reached. We noted that despite the continuation of psychological development throughout the lifetime, the deterioration of biological capacities with advancing age contribute to psychological decline. We noted the impact of declining sensory and motor capacities on opportunities for continued psychological development.

Finally, we provided an analysis as to what may be taking place when two examples of psychological decline are observed. In the case of "losing words," we focused on the actualization of stimulus functions by setting factors. In the case of intellectual activities more generally, we drew attention to the long sequences of substitutional processes operating in response-produced setting conditions.

Study Questions

1. Distinguish between biological and psychological development.
2. What is the role of biological factors in psychological events?
3. How are biological and cultural factors involved in interbehavioral history?
4. How does traditional intervention research differ from research aimed at understanding development?
5. Distinguish between biological and psychological decline in aging.

6. How do the authors explain the circumstance of "losing words" and diminished intellectual activity?

CHAPTER 12

Family Values

Although we have described cultural behavior (Kantor, 1982) in the chapter on linguistics, in this chapter we expand upon that discussion. Specifically, this chapter considers the development and evolution of values from an interbehavioral perspective. In particular, the development of values within groups, and especially family groups, is considered. Families are considered from a sociological perspective, including a description of both universal and basic interbehavioral fields in which behavior develops within family circumstances. This is followed by a consideration of families as psychological collectivities, and an outline of cultural behavior and the characteristics of such behavior. Family values are then considered specifically, including factors that influence the development and evolution of those values over time.

The Family Context

The conceptualization and study of values is central to the understanding of human behavior. People believe certain things, hold certain things to be more or less beneficial than others, and so on. While values have been considered in the context of therapeutic interventions within clinical behavior analysis (e.g., Bonow & Follette, 2009; Dahl, Plumb, Stewart, & Lundgren, 2009; Hayes, Strosahl, & Wilson, 2016; Plumb, Stewart, Dahl, & Lundgren, 2009), little attention has been given as to how values develop and evolve within groups and over the course of an individual's lifetime from a behavior analytic point of view. This chapter considers these matters from an interbehavioral perspective. It provides a foundation for the reinterpretation of existing research and generates new research questions that, in turn, may lead to novel applications. Importantly, such a foundation is also critical for the development of productive interdisciplinary relationships (see Hayes & Fryling, 2009b). Our focus is on what we will refer to as "family values," including their development, mutability, transience, and recovery over time.

We recognize that discourse on the topic of family values has had to do with what is deemed right or wrong in societal matters by virtue of religious teachings and other forms of prejudice. These discussions have pertained to such matters as gay marriage, adoption, sex education, contraception, abortion, and more (e.g., Feinberg, Wehling, Chung, Saslow, & Melvær Paulin, 2020). While we may refer to such issues as examples in this chapter, it is not our main focus. Rather, our focus is on the human family as both a societal and a psychological group in which members acquire "personalities" that align them with other members of their group and distinguish them from members of other groups. We focus more on matters of alignment than differences, with particular attention to commonly held values and beliefs. Finally, we address factors that may sustain, disrupt, or otherwise modify the latter.

Further, we recognize that a great deal has been written about the compositional structure of families, including single-parent families, two-parent families of the same or different genders, blended families, and foster families, as it relates to the practices and outcomes of childrearing (e.g., Mostafa, Gambaro, & Joshi, 2018; Santos-Nunes, Narciso, Vieira-Santos, & Roberto, 2018). Indeed, the very notion of family is evolving (e.g., Brooks, 2020; Haldeman, 2012). Expansive research programs are dedicated to understanding how different family dynamics are correlated with various outcomes, including values and other sorts of behavior. The present chapter considers family in the generic sense of a context into which children are born and raised, a type of group, regardless of its specific compositional structure. We begin by considering the family as a sociological group.

The Family as a Sociological Group

As a unit comprising more than one individual, we may look upon the family as both a sociological group and a psychological collectivity. As a sociological group, the family is a unit of persons under the auspices of which members acquire and exhibit diverse forms of behavior combining in such a way as to be recognized as their unique personalities. We are using the term "personality" to signify a person's entire repertoire of respondent and operant behavior, as well as its patterns of occurrence. As we briefly mentioned in chapter 6, these repertoires develop in the context of different fields, including those of the universal, basic, and suprabasic types (Kantor, 1924, 1982; Kantor & Smith, 1975). We elaborate upon these different types of fields here.

Universal Fields. In the earliest stages of infancy, before personality development has actually begun, the child has practically no psychological behavior. We see only simple reflexive activity coordinated with things touching its external circumstances. Kantor (1982) calls such actions "universal" in the sense that they are shared by all members of the species, a circumstance predicated on the premise that their occurrences are due to the biological characteristics of the human organism in contact with the natural properties of stimulus objects. They are, in this sense, "acquired" by particular organisms when they make contact with objects having these properties, not as a matter of

enculturation by specific groups. These types of reactions are initially so simple as to be constant in their operations, with only slight changes occurring over repeated contacts with the same stimulus objects. Such reactions, in preceding the development of actions of a more complex sort, constitute a foundation for the development of the psychological personality. Moreover, they remain a part of the person's continuously developing repertoire.

Basic and Supra-Basic Fields. As soon as a child begins to have contact with surrounding objects, another type of psychological activity begins to develop. These actions, which Kantor (1982) categorizes as "basic," are adjustments to the natural properties of surrounding stimulus objects and circumstances. Among the earliest of these are reactions of the protective, defensive, and expressive sorts. Reactions of these sorts are acquired under the auspices of particular groups and, for this reason, they are not held in common for all members of the human species. Rather, their number and variety depend directly on the numbers and kinds of objects and conditions with which a given individual has been in contact. And because no two individuals, even in the same family, can have precisely the same contacts with surrounding objects and conditions, individuals acquire and perform different basic actions. Kantor suggests that "since basic responses differ so appreciably in reactional character, they constitute the foundation for individual differences of every variety" (1982, pp.5–6).

Moreover, basic reactions acquired in early life history impact the subsequent development of more complex behaviors. This is to say that basic conduct is not only the product of the individual's earliest history, but it is also in a genuine sense a determiner of the individual's subsequent behavioral development. For example, elementary preferences for and dislikes of stimulus objects introduced by adults become elaborated into complex choice and discrimination patterns as the child matures. This latter elaboration of preferences and patterns is an example of the suprabasic category of behavior in Kantor's (1982) analysis.

We may summarize at this point by saying that while the circumstances of a particular family as a sociological group are not relevant to the exhibition of an infant's universal reactions, they are relevant to the development of a child's basic reactions and their elaboration into more complex forms of activity. Any number and combination of sociological factors may play into the number and variety of stimuli to which an infant has contact. A particular infant's contact with their surrounds may be associated with the number of other children in the family; the number of extended family members; the child's birth order; and the age, education, psychological well-being, and socioeconomic status of the parents; and on and on. Indeed, entire lines of research are dedicated to exploring these relationships (e.g., Ben-Itzchak, Nachshon, & Zachor, 2019; Carlson & Corcoran, 2001). The point here is simply that the answer to the oft-raised question "How could two members of the same family be so different?" is that they have had different experiences. The following section considers the family unit as a psychological collectivity.

The Family as a Psychological Collectivity

This section focuses on the psychological features of individuals in groups, specifically family groups. This analysis is derived from Kantor's analysis of cultural behavior more generally, which is where we begin.

Cultural Behavior. As we have considered how the repertoires or personalities of a given family's members are necessarily different, we now consider that they may also be alike in some respects. Family members' personalities may be alike in what Kantor (1982) calls their cultural conduct. Kantor (1982, p.164) describes psychological events of the cultural sort as involving arbitrary response forms coordinated with attributed properties of stimuli. Cultural response forms are considered arbitrary in the sense that they are not dependent on the physical properties of stimulus objects; they may take any form. Moreover, these arbitrary responses occur with respect to nonphysical properties of stimuli, properties that have been *attributed* to them and are thereby conventional within a particular group. Cultural stimulus functions and their coordinated arbitrary response forms are acquired under the auspices of specific groups, through the process of enculturation. The distinctiveness of psychological events of the cultural sort pertains to these events being arbitrary and conventional within groups, and developing and evolving specifically within those groups (see Kantor, 1982, p.164). We may examine the relevant features of psychological events of the cultural sort for present purposes.

First, we have discussed universal, basic, and suprabasic forms of conduct up to this point. In these types of conduct we suggested that responses are coordinated with stimulation arising from the bare qualities and conditions of things as physical objects, and that the forms of these responses are, thereby, suited to those qualities. In other words, both stimulus and response functions of the universal and basic types are determined by the object properties of stimuli.

As discussed in previous chapters, only *some* of the functional properties of stimuli inhere in their bare qualities and conditions as physical objects, though. Other properties of stimuli are attributed to them independently of their natural properties by way of verbal action. That is, some of the functional properties of stimuli are assigned to them, such as when members of a group describe them or otherwise respond with respect to them in similar ways. As addressed previously, the forms of our linguistic actions are of this sort. Likewise, properties of *beauty* or *virtue* or *value* may be attributed to things or circumstances, which have nothing whatsoever to do with the natural properties of those things.

While the formal properties of cultural responses are not determined by the natural properties of stimulus objects, the stimulus functions with which they *are* coordinated operate similarly for particular groups of people. As Kantor (1982) puts it, the stimulus functions are institutionalized within particular groups. This is to say that cultural responses are conventional within, or characteristic of, a particular group of people. Cultural stimulus functions are shared among a group of people. Languages and dialects within languages stand out as obvious examples of cultural behavior.

Further, cultural behaviors do not arise by accident or coincidence. On the contrary, their acquisition depends on a deliberate process of enculturation in the context of specific group circumstances. The emphasis on specific group circumstances here is important. It speaks to the fact that cultural behavior varies from group to group. In the present context, we may say it varies from family to family. For example, whether or not a family formally sits at a table to eat a meal, or prays before consuming food, may be considered examples of particular family practices.

Finally, the group of which we are speaking in the case of cultural behavior is not a sociological but rather a psychological group, or "collectivity" (Kantor, 1982, p.269). Membership in a psychological collectivity is defined by engaging in common action with respect to institutionalized stimulus functions whereby if you act the same as others with respect to attributed stimulus functions, you are members of the same psychological collectivity. If you don't, you aren't, despite the fact that you may still be a member of the same sociological family. Consistent with previous examples, one may be a part of a family group but not pray before meals like others in the family do. In this sense, the individual may be a part of the family in a sociological sense, but not be a part of the psychological collectivity. Differences of opinion with respect to various topics (e.g., politics) may represent other instances in which individuals are members of a sociological but not a psychological family unit.

Intrinsic Characteristics of Cultural Behavior. Cultural behavior has a number of characteristics that are particularly relevant to present concerns (Kantor, 1982). First, as just alluded to in the mention of beliefs and values as attributed functions of stimuli, cultural responses are *artificial* in the sense that they may be wholly incommensurate with events as actually experienced. For example, what is held to be good for one's health may not in fact be good for one's health. Likewise, believing in the power of voodoo to bring harm to someone despised does not actually result in harm being done, and rain does not actually fall as a consequence of dancing.

Second, cultural responses are notoriously *inconsistent* even within the same cultural system. For example, a person who, with passionate belief in the right to life abhors abortion, may at the same time be a champion of capital punishment. Indeed, this very example may be exemplified by some political groups, where such inconsistency may even be the norm. As Kantor (1982, p.171) notes, "In observing comparative cultural reactions to stimulus objects we always find a riot of inconsistencies with respect to beliefs, attitudes, customs and other practices."

Third, despite the fact that cultural responses are arbitrary, artificial, and inconsistent, they appear to be relatively stable. Although particular cultural responses may disappear for reasons to be discussed below, while they exist in a particular cultural system they remain relatively unchanged. One outcome of the stability of cultural behaviors is the conflict it creates between individuals. The more rigid one's own way of behaving, the more strange another's way of doing things appears to be. Consider cultural behaviors related to foods eaten, practices regarding marriage or death, or the treatment of the elderly as examples.

Having considered cultural behavior, including some of its various characteristics in some detail, we may turn to the topic of family values in particular. Within this general consideration we will also explore factors that contribute to the evolution of family values over time.

Stability and Change of Family Values

To make what we have said so far relevant to the topic of family values, we must consider what we mean by values, and there are two possibilities. The value of thing may be intrinsic to it in the sense that relevant stimulus functions inhere in the natural properties of that thing. In such cases, the value of a thing is a matter of its suitability or utility for a particular purpose. For example, to reach a book on a high shelf, a chair has the value of a ladder (Kantor, 1953, 1982).

The other possibility is that value stimulus functions are attributed to things under the auspices of particular collective circumstances. It is the latter that is relevant to our argument. Valuing as cultural behavior means that our beliefs as to whether things or circumstances are good or bad, right or wrong, proper or improper, are held in common with other members of our psychological collectivity despite the fact that such functions have been attributed to these things or circumstances independently of their natural properties. In other words, as described above, valuing as cultural behavior is arbitrary and artificial.

Cultural value functions may inhere in child-rearing practices (as described by Hayes et al., 1994). For example, the roles of children in a family, including how many children are thought to be preferred in any given family, pertain to cultural value functions. Having many children may be held to be good in one collectivity, whereas in another group this may be viewed as bad or irresponsible. Issues related to social, political, and economic situations also pertain to cultural value functions. In one collectivity it may be the case that relationships with others are viewed as most important, whereas in another one's possessions may be considered to be the priority. Individuals who belong to a family collectivity don't just act alike in many ways, but they often also share cultural value functions—what we may call *family values*. The following section focuses on factors impacting the stability and persistence of cultural behavior.

Factors Influencing the Stability and Persistence of Cultural Behavior

Kantor (1982) suggests that the constancy of cultural conduct may be due to its being performed by numbers of people, the implication being that the larger the number of individuals participating in the performance, the greater its stability. Cultural behaviors acquired and organized in accord with ethnic circumstances, for example, are highly stable and persistent.

The stability and persistence of cultural behavior is also impacted by the nature of the stimuli in which institutional functions inhere (Kantor, 1982). Vague or intangible institutions, especially when the origins of those functions are unknown to responders, are among the most persistent. Among such institutions, for example, are the Ten Commandments, the Golden Rule, the Cardinal Virtues, and the Seven Deadly Sins. These institutions appear to exist apart from and independently of the members of a collectivity yet have an overpowering influence on their cultural conduct. In keeping with this notion, ignorance concerning an institution's establishment plays a role: The less the individuals of a group know about the institution's origins, the more solidly ensconced it appears to be.

Factors Impacting Modification and Elimination of Cultural Behavior

The relative permanency of cultural behavior follows from the constancy of social institutions and human circumstances. As previously mentioned, religious behaviors associated with race, ethnicity, nationality, or other large group phenomena are more permanent than those associated with institutions to which fewer individuals respond in like ways. Still, despite its rigorous patterning and formality, cultural conduct, like all human phenomena, is temporary and transient. In short, cultural conduct is not immutable.

In this regard, it may be helpful to consider that persons are members of multiple collectivities, both simultaneously and serially. To a very large extent, modifications in particular types of cultural conduct occur by way of individuals enculturated in one collectivity coming into contact with those enculturated in another. When a family migrates to new societal circumstances, as when it moves from a rural to an urban region of the country or immigrates to a new county, its members inevitably acquire conventional behavior ongoing in the new circumstances. And when sufficient numbers of families do so, the cultural behaviors of the previously existing group may begin to conform to those of the newly arrived.

Changes in cultural behavior are not only inevitable outcomes of changes in one's life circumstances. They may also be deliberately imposed, with accompanying sanctions for failure to conform. A person marrying into a large extended family exhibiting different cultural behaviors may be subject to such imposition. Further, because sanctions are more readily applied to overt behaviors than to beliefs, it is overt behavior that is most likely to change by these means. Hence, the newly wed member learns to dress properly, speak properly, eat properly, and so on within a relatively short period of time. However, their cultural behaviors of the belief and value type, hidden or disguised to avoid sanctions, may persist for a much longer period of time. Still, even these more subtle behaviors are likely to be modified over an extended period of interactions with the new family collective.

Circumstances of these sorts may be encountered by students enculturated in religious families when they pursue training in the natural sciences. Cultural behaviors of the belief and value type in the new collectivity (i.e., the training program) are rather odd in that they tend to stand in stark opposition to those derived from religious traditions. As in the example of the newly wed, sanctions for failure to comply may be applied, both explicitly and implicitly. As to be expected, students' cultural behaviors, even of the belief and value variety, are often modified, or at least seem to be so.

However, cultural behavior is not just partially mutable under changing sets of circumstances; it is also transient and possible of recovery. Hence, when students who have developed conventional behaviors as natural scientists graduate, they are likely to find themselves ensconced in collective circumstances more like those of their youth. For example, they may find partners, have children, and take those children to the same churches and temples to which they themselves were taken. Bear in mind that membership in a *psychological* collectivity is a matter of engaging in common actions with respect to institutionalized stimulus functions. If you act as others act with respect to such stimulus functions, you are a member of the same psychological collectivity as those others. If you don't, you aren't. Cultural behavior not only evolves but may also recover, as one's involvement in various collectivities changes over time.

Summary and Key Points

We may conclude by reiterating some of our main themes in this chapter: Cultural behaviors, especially those of the belief and value sort, are pervasive throughout the lives of human beings. Cultural behaviors are involved in numerous social issues throughout the world and are sources of group conflict, policy debates, and more. Such behavior is indeed arbitrary in form, artificial, and inconsistent. Beliefs and values are also notoriously impervious to the onslaught of logic, and are relatively stable in form and persistent over time. This sort of cultural behavior is a dominant feature of our personalities: When one reacts culturally, one does what one's group does rather than what the circumstances require. For those interested in the preservation of the collectivity, this is a preferred outcome.

In this chapter we have focused on a particular area of beliefs and values, what we have broadly described as *family values*. Family values are a special case of a collective context where values develop and may be considered in both sociological and psychological perspectives. Taking an interbehavioral approach to the topic of family values, and in particular to how family values develop and evolve over time, expands the comprehensiveness of the discipline of behavior analysis. The interbehavioral approach to the topic of family values also provides a foundation for the interpretation of existing research on this topic, and may serve to foster meaningful interdisciplinary relations with the sciences of sociology and cultural anthropology (Hayes & Fryling, 2009b).

Study Questions

1. In what ways is a family a sociological group?

2. Distinguish between universal and basic fields as they pertain to behavioral development.

3. How is a family a psychological collectivity and how is this distinguished from a family as a sociological group?

4. Explain *family values* using your own example.

5. Describe two factors that influence cultural behavior, including that related to family values.

CHAPTER 13

Morality

We conclude this text by elaborating on our previous work on the topic of morality and ethics (Hayes et al., 1994; Hayes & Tarbox, 2007). This chapter is a fitting end to our text as it brings us back to the core premises of interbehaviorism. Conventionally understood, morality may be thought of as a set of principles pertaining to conduct deemed good or right as opposed to bad or wrong, along with the sources of or reasons for this judgment. As we may imagine, morality is not a topic upon which only a curious few have commented. The topic of morality has been a central focus of philosophical discourse for centuries, and given that so many have commented on morality we might question the value of continuing to talk about it.

In our view, the answer to this question has to do with practical affairs. It has to do with what we might consider moral action—a matter that is without recourse as long as conventional views of morality persist. Our first task, then, is to examine the logic of conventional views of morality, along with their implications for practical action. Following a discussion of conventional views, we consider behavioral, including interbehavioral, alternatives to conventional approaches to morality.

Conventional Views of Morality

The task of examining the logic of conventional views of morality is not as daunting as centuries of dialogue and scholarship on the topic might suggest. As we see it, there are only a small number of variants. The differences among them pertain to one or the other or both of two central issues. The first of these is the source of the evaluative judgment; the second concerns the permanence of that judgment. We begin with perspectives derived from absolutistic logic.

Transcendental Absolutism

The dominant position in most cultures, historically and contemporaneously, is what we may call the transcendental view of morality. Proponents of this view argue that what is "right" and "wrong" have their sources in a deity of some sort who communicates these values in the form of commandments and rules pertaining to good and bad actions, along with the eternal consequences of obedience or its failure. From this perspective, individuals are presumed to become informed of these commandments and rules by those who are thought to have special relations with the deity, among whom are prophets, priests, pastors, politicians, and the like. Even in the absence of these mediators, people may have inherent knowledge of right and wrong by way of their own special relations with the deity. Such relations are sometimes encapsulated by the presumption that the deity resides within a person's soul. As to the permanence of the deity's judgments, it is everlasting. That is, the rules of the deity apply, unchanged, for all time.

Transcendental absolutists maintain that were it not for the deity's guidance, there would be no knowledge of right and wrong. In the absence of such guidance people would do terrible things. The society would be doomed. That is, faith in the deity and trust in the deity's messages and rules are necessary for the well-being of the individual and for civilization as a whole.

As we mentioned at the beginning of the chapter, the practical implications of the various conceptualizations of morality are important to consider. According to the variant just discussed, practical problems are thought to be able to be resolved by following the deity's pronouncements more closely. If something is going well, it is thought to be a result of a close relationship. Likewise, if something is wrong, improved relations with the deity are recommended. The practical implications are simple and straightforward.

Secular Absolutism

One alternative to the transcendental absolutistic view of morality is what we may call the "secular absolutistic view." According to Zuckerman (2015), George Jacob Holyoke first coined "secularism" in 1852. Zuckerman quotes Holyoke's 1896 publication as follows (p.13):

> Secularism is a code of duty pertaining to this life, founded on considerations partly human, and intended mainly for those who find theology indefinite, or inadequate, unreliable or unbelievable. Its essential principles are three: 1) The improvement of this life by material means. 2) That science is the available providence of man. 3) That it is good to do good. Whether there be other good or not, the good of the present life is good, and it is good to seek that good.

Moral absolutists of the secular type have tended to identify a particular standard as to what is "good." For example, "self-realization" for Plato, "happiness" for Aristotle, "good will" for Kant, "greatest good for the greatest number" for Mill and Bentham (as described by Kantor, 1981, p.160). Moral absolutists of the transcendental variety are less clear about this. Their standard of goodness appears to be something along the lines of general obedience to authority.

The position of secular absolutism may sound reasonable at first glance. However, we need to consider Zuckerman's more contemporary perspective on secular morality in further detail. First, we consider the source or authority as to what is "good" or "right," "bad" or "wrong," if not an all-knowing deity. Essentially, Zuckerman's argument is that the fundamental principle of secular moralism is the Golden Rule: Do unto others as you would have them do unto you. It is an adage as old as discussions of morality have been around, and it is extremely widespread. Zuckerman (2015, p.14) cites the following evidence of adherence to this principle:

> In Egypt as early as 600BCE: "That which you would hate to be done to you, do not do to another."
>
> In China by Confucius (551–479BCE): "Do not impose upon others what you would not desire others to impose upon you." And, "What you would require of your friend, first apply in your treatment of him."
>
> In Greece, Thales (624–546BCE) argued that humans live most virtuously and justly when "we never do ourselves what we blame in others."
>
> In ancient Israel by Hillel (1st century BCE): "What is hateful to you, do not do to another."
>
> And all of these entreaties predate the Gospels of Jesus wherein it is said: "All

things whatsoever ye would that men should do to you, do ye even so to them."

The Golden Rule speaks to social relations. Adherents of the Golden Rule suggest that our knowledge of "right" and "wrong," and therein the guidance afforded for "good" and "bad" conduct, is derived from our day-to-day interactions with others. In short, morality does not require instruction from an all-knowing deity. It is, instead, a matter of basic human empathy. And, inasmuch as human empathy is held to be a constant of human life, Golden Rule secularists are absolutistic.

The sources of morality from a secular perspective are somewhat more complicated than this, of course. Moreover, secular morality is not all of one piece, its variants evident in their different source claims. First, though, it is noteworthy that what secularists have in common is their contention that morality does not require a deity, and to substantiate this contention they cite some interesting findings. As previously mentioned, transcendentalists claim that without guidance from a deity, unwitting people would do terrible things and societies would be doomed. With respect to the morality of individual people, Hall and colleagues (2009, as cited in Zuckerman, 2015) examined the relationship between religiosity and racism. They found that people who were more religious were more likely to hold racists views. Other studies (cited in Zuckerman, 2015) have shown this same relationship on such matters as government use of torture, the death penalty, military aggression, and nationalism.

By contrast, secularists were more likely to support measures to deal with climate change than their religious counterparts. They were also more likely to support women's equality and to protect the civil liberties of same-sex couples. They were more likely to be opposed to the corporal punishment of children, and showed greater concern for the mistreatment of animals. In sum, in Zuckerman's (2015, p.22) words, "when it comes to a host of issues and positions—from torture to war, from global warming to the welfare of animals—secular people clearly feel that it is good to do good in this known lifetime."

Secular moralists also comment on the goodness of society in the absence of a deity. On the basis of numerous international surveys, countries have been sorted into two groups: those with the highest rates of God belief and those with the highest rates of atheism, agnosticism, and theological indifference, with the aim then being able to compare the groups on a number of indices of societal well-being. If we were to follow the logic of the transcendental absolutists, the more religious countries should fare better on generally agreed-upon measures of societal well-being. This was not the outcome of this assessment, as indicated by Zuckerman (2015, p.46):

> Rather it is those countries with the lowest rates of God belief that tend to be the "healthiest" in terms of prosperity, equality, freedom, democracy, women's rights, human rights, educational attainment, crime rates, life expectancy, and so forth (though not all, to be sure, such as Vietnam and China), and it is those nations with the highest rates of God belief that tend to be relatively unsuccessful in terms of any standard sociological measurements of societal health—from having high infant mortality rates to high poverty rates, from entrenched inequality to a stubborn degree of corruption, from lack of clean water to absence of democracy.

And, on almost every other measure of societal goodness, including "happiness," the least religious countries fare substantially better than the most religious countries.

It is important to note that secular moralists are not claiming that religiosity is causally responsible for societal depravity or that its opposite is causally responsible for societal well-being. Their point is, simply, that societal goodness, like personal goodness, does not depend on belief in a deity. Indeed, it is possible to do good without belief in a deity, and more importantly for secularists, it is good to do so. In other words, while a deity may not be needed to do good, it is still inherently good to do good things.

With this behind us, we may return to the sources of goodness claimed by secular moralists of various types. Earlier, we suggested that the differences among them had to do with their source claims. In other words, the differences pertain to where knowledge of "right" and "wrong" comes from. Upon further review, it turns out that morality is not merely held to be an outcome of our day-to-day interactions with other people; it is also attributable to multiple factors and forces encapsulated in different scientific domains, among them cultural anthropology, sociology, biology, and psychology. Much of this discussion is aligned with a natural science perspective, including the evolution and codification of cultural practices over time and the current organization and operations of societal groups, including the family. And, of factors in both of these domains, there is an emphasis on relative security and stability as essential for sustained moral action. Moral actions of societal groups, whatever their sources, are sustained in stable societal circumstances. Unstable societal conditions, such as war, alter routine social practices whereupon conventional behavior of all types, including those of the moral sort, may be disturbed.

Confidence in this analysis wanes when biological factors and forces are added to the account, however. That is, when various fleshy parts and pieces, among them neurons, hormones, and genes, are held to make a contribution to morality. These biological factors are sometimes considered to be more than mere contributions to moral actions, but rather to be their causes.

Regrettably, the secularity in many versions of this general position does not run deep. In fact, what is lost in eliminating an omnipotent deity is found again in an exalted view of the human being. In other words, the individual person may be held to be the source of goodness. Thus, moral action, or goodness, is held to be a matter of personal responsibility, the capacity for reason, and the will to do the right thing. Moreover, because it is a matter of personal responsibility and willfulness, rightful conduct is deserving of a society's praise and reward, wrongful conduct of its blame and punishment. This is to say that the practical implication of the secular absolutist approach is that problems may be thought to be a result of poor character, failing to take responsibility, or insufficient concern for the greater good.

Following from this, the problem to be solved becomes one of finding ways to improve people's character in this regard, by developing a better "moral compass," for example. Another implication of this view is that people may be blamed for their failures to act according to what is deemed good even though these practices may not produce the aforementioned desired change in character.

We have considered two absolutistic positions on the topic of morality, the transcendental and the secular, including their limitations as far as practical implications go. We turn now to perspectives on morality derived from the philosophical stance of relativism.

Secular Relativism

While secular perspectives are similar in that they share the conviction that moral action does not require instruction from a deity, they are not all the same. Indeed, we have just commented on the premises of secular absolutism, but not all secularists are absolutists. Some secularists are decidedly relativistic (Zuckerman, 2015). Secular relativists, like their absolutist counterparts, argue that knowledge of right and wrong is acquired over the course of a person's experiences as a member of a culture. However, relativists maintain that there are no stable criteria by which the rightfulness or wrongfulness of conduct may be judged. Rather, what falls into these categories amounts to whatever meets the needs of a particular group at a particular moment in time. As such, whatever might be right for a particular group at any given time might not be right for another group at that time, and similarly, what is right for any given group at one time may not be at another time (Hayes & Tarbox, 2007).

Further, to assert that the source of moral knowledge is the culture does not necessarily mean that the culture is also the source of control over moral action. Instead, generally speaking, relativistic moralists assume that once knowledge of right and wrong is derived from cultural sources, it prevails thereafter as a personal possession available for consultation on future occasions in which matters of morality are at issue. This is to say, once what is deemed right or wrong is established within the context of a group, the subsequent engagement in rightful or wrongful conduct is held to be knowingly and willfully done by individual members of the group. As such, the practical implication of this position is similar to that of secular absolutists: It remains the individual's responsibility for continuing to act in a way that is deemed to be relatively good in any given circumstance within a particular cultural group.

In summary, recall that the reason we thought it was important to continue to talk about morality, despite its having been a topic of discourse for thousands of years, had to do with practical affairs. As we have described, the problem with notions like inherited tendencies, good and bad brain wiring, personal responsibility and free will is that you can't do much about it. That is, as far as practical implications go, traditional ways of approaching the topic of morality aren't all that helpful. We turn now to behavioral alternatives.

Morality from a Naturalistic Perspective

Not all secular positions find themselves in the predicament of those described in the previous sections, including those of B.F. Skinner (e.g., 1971) and J. R Kantor (e.g., 1981). We may begin by noting that the views of Skinner and Kantor on this topic are differently focused. Skinner (1971) focuses on the standard by which actions may be judged as "good." It is an absolute standard. By contrast, Kantor (1981) focuses on the actions themselves, including their participating factors and unique configurations. Kantor does not isolate a standard of goodness. Consequently, a straightforward comparison of the two positions is not readily made. Our plan is to describe Skinner's position first, with an emphasis on his standard of goodness. After this, we will explain why no such standard is present in Kantor's work. We will conclude with some cautionary remarks about the all-important matter of practical action.

Skinner's Position

Skinner (1971) articulates an absolute standard of moral goodness, that being survival. Basically, Skinner's analysis on this issue is that whatever promotes survival is considered to be good, whereas whatever makes survival less likely is considered to be bad. Here, the survival metaphor is borrowed from biology, where it is used in descriptions of evolution, and Skinner applies it to both individual behavior and the behavior of groups. Specifically, Skinner distinguishes among cases of behaving for the good of oneself, the good of others, and the good of the culture. We now briefly distinguish between these cases as pertinent to our overall analysis of morality.

In Skinner's perspective, behaving for the good of oneself involves behavior that promotes the survival of the individual. In the absence of other factors, individuals will naturally engage in behavior that promotes the survival of themselves as individual members of a species. This is not the case of behaving for the good of others or for the good of the culture. Behaving in these ways requires instruction or intervention from the group. Behavior that promotes the survival of oneself may not promote the survival of others or the culture, whereby it is subject to suppression by the group. This is to say, in Skinner's view, behaving for the good of others involves behavior that is reinforced by intentional action on the parts of others so as to enhance the likelihood of their survival.

It is important to note here that behaving for the good of others is not derived from some hypothetical character trait or a priori knowledge, as is the case for secular absolutists. The implication of Skinner's analysis is that people who behave for the good of others do so because their behavior is reinforced by contingencies arranged by other people.

Finally, an even higher level of moral behavior is described by Skinner as behaving for the good of the culture. Here, individuals are not behaving for the good of themselves, or even for the good of others who are deliberately arranging contingencies for such behavior, but for the good (survival) of the culture. Behavior for the good of the culture is reinforced and supported by verbal stimuli, including rules and practices shared among members of the group. Skinner notes that this progression of behaving for the good of oneself, others, and the culture involves behavior coming under the control of increasingly remote consequences by way of present social and cultural stimulation.

The practical implications of Skinner's analysis of morality warrants further consideration. To reiterate, according to Skinner, whatever promotes survival is good, and whatever diminishes or threatens it is bad. Survival, as a standard of goodness, is derived from biological considerations as to the evolution of the species. That is, whatever characteristics have fostered the survival of the species are carried forward, and whatever hasn't doesn't. Survival, as such, speaks to the organismic conditions and environing circumstances that may have fostered this outcome. It is an outcome concept, not a new kind of cause as Skinner would have it (1971).

Accordingly, whatever behavior may have contributed to the survival of the individual and hence the species in the past, such as a susceptibility to sugar and fat as reinforcers, may not promote the continuing survival of the individual. This applies to cultural practices too. This is to say, whatever practices are thought to have been important to the survival of others or of the culture at earlier points may or may not continue to be so. Furthermore, the processes of evolution we are describing here occur at an especially slow pace (over the course of generations of a species or generations of a culture). As such, it becomes especially difficult to imagine the participation of contributing conditions.

For these reasons, the value of Skinner's standard of goodness for practical action is questionable. What does the selection metaphor help us do? How does it help us understand what's good, right now? In other words, because the circumstances in which both individual behavior and cultural practices occur are continuously changing and multifactored, it is not possible to know, at any given moment, what would be more or less likely to promote future survival at either level. In short, survival doesn't tell us what we should do or should promote in any given situation. It is, rather, a descriptive explanation of how what is might have come to be. More pointedly, from a scientific perspective, there is neither purpose nor direction in evolution. There is only change. In this light, it is only a measure of change that could conceivably constitute a workable process alternative to Skinner's outcome concept of survival. This is where Kantor's interbehavioral position may be especially helpful.

Kantor's Position

Kantor's (1981) work on the topic of morality is focused on the nature of moral actions as a distinct category of interbehavior. While there is much to be gained by examining Kantor's analysis of moral action in detail, we focus here on matters that are pertinent to explaining why a standard of goodness is missing from his formulation.

Kantor (1981, p.167) takes the position that because moral behavior is a type of psychological interbehavior, a model of moral situations symbolizes a special type of psychological field. The focus of a psychological field of the moral type, as of any type, is an interaction of behaving and stimulating (chapter 3). Its distinguishing features include the presence of a verbally competent behaving person, stimulus objects or events harboring value functions, acts of choosing among possible alternatives, and the setting or auspices under which moral interactions occur. We review each of these features below.

The Behaving Person. Of the behaving person, Kantor argues that "human beings are not only biological organisms but civil or social beings also" (1981, p.103). Eliminated by this interpretation are all sorts of supernatural faculties and powers such as the mind or soul, a priori knowledge of right and wrong, and the freedom of the will. The mention that humans are social or civil beings is a reference to the observation that "mankind has also undergone another and different evolution so that human organisms are capable of performing behavior not possible for their biological cousins" (1981, p.103). They display an evolution that makes them cultural organisms. "They have evolved to the point of being talking animals ... building for themselves various forms of cultural institutions in the form of social organizations, laws, technologies, language systems, literatures, religions, moralities, and philosophies" (Kantor, 1981, p.104). Moreover, the characteristics just mentioned are all evolved in the lifetimes of particular individuals. "[E]verything that happens to the individual consists of contacts with things or events during which the individual develops traits or modes of action constituting his reactional biography, while the things or events he encounters take on functions of stimulation" (Kantor, 1981, p.102).

•

Value Functions of Stimuli. Contrary to more traditional notions, Kantor (1982) argues that "values are not additional or epiphenomenal to circumstances of everyday existence. They are functional in every respect and [are] not to be set aside or above events" (p.320). This is to say, "valuing" is just one of the many actions a given object or event may stimulate. He further distinguishes between intrinsic and attributed value functions. Intrinsic value functions are those inherent in the natural properties of a stimulus object, which is to say they exist independently of a person's verbal attributions. Hayes and colleagues (1994, p.14) describe examples of this: "For example, to pound a tent peg into the ground, a rock has the value of a hammer. To reach a book on a high shelf, a chair has the value of a ladder." Hayes and colleagues (1994, p.14) contrast this with attributed value functions: In their words, attributed value functions are "verbally imposed upon stimulus objects by persons, without whom they would not exist or operate." Value functions of the latter sort are involved in moral fields.

•

Choosing Among Alternatives. All conceptions of choice involve the presence of alternatives in some way. Accordingly, for Kantor, choice implies a circumstance in which there is reason to believe that more than one response might be performed with respect to a given stimulus object, or that more than one stimulus function might be operative from that source. In Kantor's view, choosing acts are complex responses involving two distinct phases, one of which is an implicit field of interaction involving substitute stimulation with respect to anticipated consequences. The second phase involves taking action based upon the perception of the likely consequences. There is no "freedom" of choice entailed in the analysis. (It should be noted that not all behavior situations involve choosing acts, and not all acts of choosing are moral in type; Hayes et al., 1994.) In sum, what distinguishes a moral choice from a choice of other sorts is the nature of the implicit actions occurring with respect to the consequences of alternative courses of action. It is only when these are valuative in type, that is, when our responses to such are to find them good or bad, right or wrong, are choosing acts considered moral.

Setting or Auspices. The problem posed by the insinuation of group membership in a definition of individual morality, as suggested by Skinner, is reconciled in Kantor's psychological formulation by the construct of cultural behavior. Kantor classifies behavior on the basis of its distribution across members of a species and the conditions of its occurrence or acquisition. As described in the previous chapter, behavior may be said to be universal, meaning that it is shared by all members of a species with respect to a particular stimulus situation. Unconditional stimulus-response relations are of this sort. Another class of behaviors is acquired or learned over the course of an individual organism's historical interactions with particular stimulating conditions. These repertoires, while possibly similar to the repertoires of other individuals by virtue of common conditions of their development, are not explicitly shared but are rather unique to the individual. Another class, the cultural class, includes actions that are both shared (though not universally across a species) and learned (though not in the absence of explicit instruction). Behavior functions of the cultural type are interrelated with attributed functions of stimuli that have become institutionalized in the context of particular sociological groups. They are nonetheless actions of individuals, actions acquired under the auspices of a particular group that serve to identify individuals as members of that group. They are not actions of groups; actions of groups are not the subject matter of a science of psychology.

We now consider what this means, and what it has to do with the absence of a standard of goodness in Kantor's formulation. Remember that Kantor's philosophy of interbehaviorism (e.g.,

1950, 1953) as well as his system of interbehavioral psychology (e.g., 1958) is devoid of causality except as this concept is taken to refer to the totality of factors comprising an integrated field. The latter is a way of pointing to the historicity of the present field. It is a way of saying that causality is nothing more or less than all that continues to be occurring. What this means in a psychological context is that we are our histories of interactions with our environs. We are at any moment understandable as a point in the continuous evolution of those interactions. What we do at any moment is the only thing we can do, we cannot do otherwise, we do what we do. Important for present purposes is that the same construction may be applied to events of the biological and cultural domains. They are at this moment their histories of interactions. They are as they are. They could not be otherwise, and we can therefore not say what they should be. Looked at in this way, nothing can be said to be good or bad, right or wrong, as a categorical imperative. There are no absolutes or universals.

By contrast, dichotomous categories of good and bad are required when the aims of a scientific formulation are prediction and, more specifically, control. Exerting control or influence over current actions so as to produce remote outcomes deemed "good" implies, first, a specification as to what is good, and second, a capacity to predict the achievement of that good by those actions. Neither is required in the absence of these scientific aims.

In making this analysis, the practical implications of Kantor's analysis of moral behavior becomes an issue. We are still left with the question of what we should do—the topic of moral *action* with which we began this chapter. Kantor's (1981) analysis does not tell us what we *should* do in any particular situation. As we have described in this chapter, Kantor's analysis actually dismisses this question entirely. Sciences are descriptive enterprises. This is not to dismiss the fact that moral action is taken, but rather to acknowledge that the question of what we *should* do in any particular situation isn't an entirely scientific question. The value of Kantor's (1981) analysis of this issue is to draw attention to the factors participating in moral action, including our histories of interaction with stimulating conditions. That is, rather than attempt to prescribe an analysis of what is good, Kantor turns us toward a psychological analysis of moral actions themselves. To us, an analysis of moral actions themselves is the focus of a natural science of psychology, and something that Kantor's work has much to offer.

Summary and Key Points

We conclude by considering again why we might want to address the topic of morality given that it has been the subject of philosophical discourse for eons. On the matter of morality, nothing of scientific worth or practical utility is to be gained by adherence to transcendental absolutism. A little more worth, though no more utility, comes from secular relativism. More scientific worth, and some utility, may be gained by alignment with secular absolutism of the sort Skinner espouses. And, finally, of Kantor's position, we would argue that its scientific worth is its utility.

Study Questions

1. Explain the transcendental absolutism approach to morality.
2. What is the difference between secular absolutism and transcendental absolutism?
3. Distinguish between secular relativism and secular absolutism.
4. What are the fundamentals of Skinner's approach to moral behavior?
5. Describe Kantor's interbehavioral approach to moral behavior.

Conclusion

Our primary aim in writing this book was to share our knowledge of Kantor's philosophical and psychological works in such a way that they might be more accessible to readers relatively unfamiliar with Kantor's contributions to behavior science. As we described in the early chapters of the book, the philosophy of interbehaviorism provides a detailed foundation for the science of behavior as it is now and may become in the future. We have made the case that a valid, significant, and comprehensive natural science of behavior does not emerge accidentally or unwittingly. These features of a scientific enterprise are products of system building activity. System building is a set of practices designed to ensure the internal consistency of a scientific enterprise, as well as to enable it to sustain coherent relations with other sciences. Kantor's concern for the value of system building is unique in the behavior sciences: We know of no other behavioral perspective that values system building sufficiently to be explicit about its postulational framework. As we see it, to be fully committed to the natural part of a natural science of behavior is to recognize the value of system building for its outcome of eliminating dualism, reductionism, and other missteps in the way of its achievement.

We have also provided an overview of interbehavioral psychology, including the construction of its unique subject matter and its configuration as an integrated field. The field construction replaces the presumption of linear causality exploited for purposes of explanation in other branches of behavior science. Conceptualizing the subject matter of behavior science as participating factors in an interbehavioral field has implications for the analysis of many areas of work in our discipline. Some of these implications are addressed in the chapters on research and application. Specifically, we have shown how taking an interbehavioral perspective increases the likelihood of different research questions being asked. It also fosters consideration of applications pertaining to long ignored problems of history and context.

Part 2 of the book is focused on an interbehavioral approach to a number of different categories of interbehavior, among them linguistic behavior, memory, feelings, and family values. These are some of the most complicated forms of interbehavior, their complications arising from the participation of substitute stimulation and implicit responses. An additional feature of Kantor's analysis of psychological happenings, emphasized in part 2 of the text, is that of cultural behavior. Although we considered cultural behavior in chapters on language, family values, and morality, much of the behavior of human beings is cultural in the sense that Kantor has constructed it. As such, the concept of cultural behavior is relevant to the work of behavior scientists engaged in both investigation and application.

As previously mentioned, our aim was to provide an introductory overview of interbehaviorism and interbehavioral psychology. While we have described some of the most fundamental features of Kantor's position in this book, the book is far from exhaustive. Kantor's contributions to a natural science of behavior are enormous and of exceedingly broad scope. Still, we hope to have set the stage for further study. To this end, we have included a bibliography of Kantor's published works in the appendix. We have also included in the references section some of our own works that have not been cited in the text but may be of use in further study.

Finally, we have written this book to honor the legacy of Jacob Robert Kantor. In his last book, entitled *Tragedy and the Event Continuum* (1983), Kantor defined tragedy as the truncation of potential. In this sense, Kantor's death at the age of ninety-six was not a tragedy. Little more could be expected of any one man. It would be a truncation of potential if his great works did not find their way to a new generation of behavior scientists and philosophers, though. We have written this book to avoid this tragedy.

Glossary

adjustment stimulus—the referent in a referential linguistic segment (i.e., the thing being spoken of).

auxiliary stimulus—the referee in a referential linguistic segment (i.e., the person being spoken to).

collectivity—a group of individuals who respond similarly to various things and circumstances (e.g., language and customs).

comprehensiveness—in the context of system building, this refers to the extent to which a science addresses all aspects of its identified subject matter.

contingency—describes a dependency relation. In behavior analysis, responding is dependent on its consequences.

coordination—in the context of system building, this refers to the extent to which the assumptions of its various subsystems (e.g., interpretive, investigative, and applied) cohere with one another.

disciplinary science—a scientific enterprise focused on a unique subject matter.

enculturation—the process by which an individual becomes a part of a cultural collectivity (e.g., group or family).

hypothetical construct—refers to an unobserved entity that is held to explain an observed phenomenon (e.g., mind, psyche, etc.).

implicit behavior—behavior that occurs with respect to substitute stimulation.

interbehavioral history—an individual's history of interacting with their environment.

interbehaviorism—the study of the relation of stimulating and responding.

interdisciplinary science—a scientific enterprise in which the subject matters of more than one disciplinary science are related.

media of contact—the means through which an individual is in contact with their environment (e.g., light, sound).

mediational—a type of referential behavior operating in close contact with nonlinguistic events or circumstances (i.e., some additional, nonlinguistic activity is involved).

monitorial task—a task of a philosopher of science, aimed at sustaining a coherent scientific system.

narrational—a type of referential behavior not operating in close contact with nonlinguistic events or circumstances (e.g., as in conversations).

operant behavior—a class of behavior maintained by reinforcement.

postulates—formal assumptions.

psychological event—the unit of analysis in interbehavioral psychology, composed of a multifactored integrated field.

referee—the listener in a referential linguistic segment.

referent—the thing or event to which the referrer orients the referee (i.e., the thing being spoken of).

referential behavior—a type of linguistic behavior involving bistimulation having its sources in a referee and a referent.

referrer—the speaker in a referential linguistic segment.

response function—the responding of an individual with respect to the stimulating of an object or event.

scientific system—the structure and organization of a scientific discipline.

semantic supervision—a task of a philosopher of science aimed at ensuring the consistent and proper use of technical terms.

setting factors—the situational features participating in a psychological event.

significance—in the context of system building, this refers to the coherence of a specific scientific system with the larger domain of science (i.e., more coherence with other sciences = significance).

stimulus function—the stimulating action of an object or event with respect to the responding of an individual.

stimulus object—the thing or event from which stimulation operates.

substitute stimulus—refers to stimulation operating from a non-original source as a product of its concurrence with an original source under conditions of association.

symbolic behavior—a type of linguistic behavior involving sequential stimulation. Symbolic behavior involves substitute stimulation.

system building—activities involved in the development of a science, including the articulation of its subject matter and the assumptions concerning it. Activities aimed at assuring the validity, significance, and comprehensiveness of a science.

valid and invalid philosophy—valid philosophies are derived from contacts with events, whereas invalid philosophies are derived from cultural folklore.

validity—in the context of system building, this refers to the internal consistency of a scientific system (i.e., validity = high internal consistency).

References

Atkins, P.W.B., Wilson, D.S., & Hayes, S.C. (2019). *Prosocial: Using evolutionary science to build productive, equitable, and collaborative groups.* Oakland, CA: New Harbinger.

Barnes-Holmes, D., Barnes-Holmes, Y., & McEnteggart, C. (2020a). Updating RFT (More Field than Frame) and its implications for process-based therapy. *The Psychological Record, 70*, 605–624.

Barnes-Holmes, D., Harte, C., & McEnteggart, C. (2020b). Implicit cognition and social behavior. In M. Fryling, R.A. Rehfeldt, J. Tarbox, and L. Hayes (Eds.), *Applied behavior analysis of language and cognition: Concepts and principles for practitioners* (pp.264–280). Oakland, CA: New Harbinger.

Baron-Cohen, S., Leslie, A.M., & Frith, U. (1985). Does the autistic child have a "theory of mind"? *Cognition, 21*, 37–46.

Beavers, G.A., Iwata, B.A., & Lerman, D.C. (2013). Thirty years of research on the functional analysis of problem behavior. *Journal of Applied Behavior Analysis, 46,* 1–21.

Ben-Itzchak, E., Nachshon, N., & Zachor, D.A. (2019). Having siblings is associated with better social functioning in autism spectrum disorder. *Journal of Abnormal Psychology, 47,* 921–931.

Bonow, J.T., & Follette, W.C. (2009). Beyond values clarification: Addressing client values in clinical behavior analysis. *The Behavior Analyst, 32,* 69–84.

Bourgeois, M.S. (1992). Evaluating memory wallets in conversations with persons with dementia. *Journal of Speech & Hearing Research, 35*(6), 1344–1357.

Brooks, D. (2020, March). The nuclear family was a mistake. *The Atlantic,* 54–69.

Brown, S.R. (2006). Q Methodology and naturalistic subjectivity. In B.D. Midgley and E.K. Morris (Eds.), *Modern perspectives on J.R. Kantor and interbehaviorism* (pp.251–268). Oakland, CA: Context Press.

Carlson, M.J., & Corcoran, M.E. (2001). Family structure and children's behavioral and cognitive outcomes. *Journal of Marriage and Family, 63,* 779–792.

Costa, P.A., & Biddell, M. (2017). Modern families: Parenting desire, intention, and experience among Portuguese lesbian, gay, and bisexual individuals. Journal of Family Issues, 38, 500–521.

Dahl, J.C., Plumb, J.C., Stewart, I., & Lundgren, T. (2009). *The art and science of valuing in psychotherapy: Helping clients discover, explore, and commit to action using Acceptance and Commitment Therapy.* Oakland, CA: New Harbinger.

DeBernardis, G.M., Hayes, L.J., & Fryling, M.J. (2014). Perspective taking as a continuum. *The Psychological Record, 64,* 123–131.

Delaney, P.F., & Austin, J. (1998). Memory as behavior: The importance of acquisition and remembering strategies. *The Analysis of Verbal Behavior, 15,* 75–91.

Feinberg, M., Wehling, E., Chung, J.M., Saslow, L.R., & Melvær Paulin, I. (2020). Measuring moral politics: How strict and nurturant family values explain individual differences in conservatism, liberalism, and the political middle. *Journal of Personality and Social Psychology, 118,* 777–804.

Finn, M., Barnes-Holmes, D., & McEnteggart, C. (2018). Exploring the single-trial-type-dominance effect on the IRAP: Developing a differential arbitrary applicable relational responding effects (DAARRE) model. *The Psychological Record, 68,* 11–25.

Fisher, W.W., Piazza, C.C., & Roane, H.S. (Eds.). (2021). *Handbook of applied behavior analysis* (2nd ed.). New York: The Guilford Press.

Fryling, M.J. (2011). The impact of applied behavior analysis on the science of behavior. *Behavior and Social Issues, 19,* 24–31.

Fryling, M.J. (2013a). Constructs and events in verbal behavior. *The Analysis of Verbal Behavior, 29,* 157–165.

Fryling, M.J. (2013b). Philosophy, theory, and the practice of applied behavior analysis. *European Journal of Behavior Analysis, 14,* 45–54.

Fryling, M.J. (2014). Contextual intervention for caregiver non-adherence with behavioral intervention plans. *Child & Family Behavior Therapy, 36,* 191–203.

Fryling, M.J. (2016). A developmental-behavioral analysis of lying. *International Journal of Psychology and Psychological Therapy, 16*, 13–22.

Fryling, M.J. (2017). The functional independence of Skinner's verbal operants: Conceptual and applied implications. *Behavioral Interventions, 32*, 70–78.

Fryling, M.J., & Baires, N. (2016). The practical importance of the distinction between open and closed-ended indirect assessments. *Behavior Analysis in Practice, 9*, 146–151.

Fryling, M.J., & Hayes, L.J. (2009). Psychological constructs and events: An alliance with Smith. *The Psychological Record, 59*, 133–142.

Fryling, M.J., & Hayes, L.J. (2010). An interbehavioral analysis of memory. *European Journal of Behavior Analysis, 11*, 53–68.

Fryling, M.J., & Hayes, L.J. (2011). The concept of function in the analysis of behavior. *Mexican Journal of Behavior Analysis, 37*, 11–20.

Fryling, M.J., & Hayes, L.J. (2014). An interbehavioral investigation of remembering interactions. *The Psychological Record, 64*, 1–11.

Fryling, M.J., & Hayes, L.J. (2019). Interpersonal closeness and conflict in interbehavioral perspective. *International Journal of Psychology and Psychological Therapy, 19*, 131–140.

Fryling, M., Rehfeldt, R.A., Tarbox, J., & Hayes, L.J. (Eds.). (2020). *Applied behavior analysis of language and cognition: Concepts and principles for practitioners*. Oakland, CA: New Harbinger.

Greer, R.D., Pohl, P., Du, L., & Moschella, J.L. (2020). Identification and establishment of bidirectional verbal operants. In M. Fryling, R.A. Rehfeldt, J. Tarbox, and L. Hayes (Eds.), *Applied behavior analysis of language and cognition: Concepts and principles for Practitioners* (pp.55–71). Oakland, CA: New Harbinger.

Greer, R.D., & Ross, D.E. (2008). *Verbal behavior analysis: Inducing and expanding verbal capabilities in children with language delays*. Boston: Pearson.

Greer, R.D., & Speckman, J. (2009). The integration of speaker and listener responses: A theory of verbal development. *The Psychological Record, 59*, 449–488.

Haldeman, D.C. (2012). The evolving family. In N.A. Fouad, J.A. Carter, and L.M. Subich (Eds.),

APA handbook on counseling psychology (vol.2): *Practice, interventions, and applications* (pp.105–123). Washington, DC: American Psychological Association.

Hall, D., Matz, D., & Wood, W. (2009). Why don't we practice what we preach? A meta-analytic review of religious racism. *Personality and Social Psychology Review, 14*(1), 126–139.

Hanley, G.P. (2012). Functional assessment of problem behavior: Dispelling myths, overcoming implementation obstacles, and developing new lore. *Behavior Analysis in Practice, 5*, 54–72.

Harte, C., Barnes-Holmes, Y., Barnes-Holmes, D., & McEnteggart, C. (2017). Persistent rule-following in the face of reversed reinforcement contingencies: The differential impact of direct versus derived rules. *Behavior Modification, 41*, 743–763.

Hass, A. (1984). Comment on J.R. Kantor. *The Interbehaviorist, 12*(3). University of Kansas.

Hayes, L.J. (1992a). Equivalence as process. In S.C. Hayes & L.J. Hayes (Eds.), *The international institute on verbal relations: Understanding verbal relations* (pp.97–108). Oakland, CA: Context Press.

Hayes, L.J. (1992b). The psychological present. *The Behavior Analyst, 15*(2), 139–145.

Hayes, L.J. (1993). Reality and truth. In S.C. Hayes, L.J. Hayes, H.W. Reese, & T.R. Sarbin (Eds.), *Varieties of scientific contextualism* (pp.35–44). Oakland, CA: Context Press.

Hayes, L.J. (1994). Thinking. In S.C. Hayes, L.J. Hayes, M. Sato, & K. Ono (Eds.), *Behavior analysis of language and* cognition (pp.149–164). Oakland, CA: Context Press.

Hayes, L.J. (1996). Listening with understanding and speaking with meaning. *The Journal of the Experimental Analysis of Behavior, 65*(1), 282–283.

Hayes, L.J., Adams, M.A., & Dixon, M.R. (1997). Causal constructs and conceptual confusions. *The Psychological Record, 47*, 97–112.

Hayes, L.J., Adams, M.A., & Rydeen, K.L. (1994). Ethics, choice and value. In L.J. Hayes, G.J. Hayes, S.C. Moore, & P.M. Ghezzi (Eds)., *Ethical issues in developmental disabilities* (pp.11–39). Oakland, CA: Context Press.

Hayes, L.J., Dubuque, E.M., Fryling, M.J., & Pritchard, J.K. (2009). A behavioral systems analysis of behavior analysis as a scientific system. *Journal of Organizational Behavior Management, 3–4,* 315–332.

Hayes, L.J., & Fryling, M.J. (2009a). Overcoming the pseudo-problem of private events in the analysis of behavior. *Behavior and Philosophy, 37,* 39–57.

Hayes, L.J., & Fryling, M.J. (2009b). Toward an interdisciplinary science of culture. *The Psychological Record, 59,* 679–700.

Hayes, L.J., & Fryling, M.J. (2013). Self-knowledge as interbehavior. *Conductual, 1,* 26–37.

Hayes, L.J., & Fryling, M.J. (2014). Motivation in behavior analysis: A critique. *The Psychological Record, 64,* 339–347.

Hayes, L.J., & Fryling, M.J. (2017). Feelings in psychological perspective. *European Journal of Behavior Analysis, 18,* 39–51.

Hayes, L.J., & Fryling, M.J. (2018). Psychological events as integrated fields. *The Psychological Record, 68*(4), 273–277.

Hayes, L.J., & Fryling, M.J. (2019). Functional and descriptive contextualism. *Journal of Contextual Behavior Science, 14,* 119–126.

Hayes, L.J., & Tarbox, J. (2007). Ethics and values in interbehavioral perspective. In J.W. Jacobson, A. Mulick, & J. Rojahn (Eds.), *Handbook of intellectual and developmental disabilities* (pp.691–717). New York: Springer.

Hayes, S.C., Barnes-Holmes, D., & Roche, B. (Eds.). (2001). *Relational frame theory: A post-Skinnerian account of human language and cognition.* New York: Plenum.

Hayes, S.C., & Sanford, B.T. (2014). Cooperation came first: Evolution and human cognition. *Journal of the Experimental Analysis, 101,* 112–129.

Hayes, S.C., Strosahl, K.D., & Wilson, K.G. (2012). *Acceptance and commitment therapy: The process of mindful change* (2nd ed.). New York: The Guilford Press.

Holman, G., Kanter, J., Tsai, M., & Kohlenberg, R. (2017). *Functional analytic psychotherapy made simple.* Oakland, CA: New Harbinger.

Hooker, S.A., Grigsby, M.E., Riegel, B., & Bekelman, D.B. (2015). The impact of relationship quality on health-related outcomes in heart failure patients and informal family caregivers: An integrative review. *The Journal of Cardiovascular Nursing, 30,* S52–S63.

Iwata, B.A., Kahng, S.W., Wallace, M.D., & Lindberg, J.S. (2000). The functional analysis modelof behavioral assessment. In J. Austin and J.E. Carr (Eds.), *Handbook of applied behavior analysis* (pp.61–89). Oakland, CA: Context Press.

Kanter, J., Kuczynski, A.M., Manbeck, K.E., Corey, M.D., & Wallace, E.C. (2020). An integrative contextual behavioral model of intimate relations. *Journal of Contextual Behavioral Science, 18,* 75–91.

Kantor, J.R. (1922). Memory: A triphase objective action. *Journal of Philosophy, 23,* 624–639.

Kantor, J.R. (1924, 1926). *The principles of psychology* (vol I & II). Akron, OH: Principia.

Kantor, J.R. (1936). *An objective psychology of grammar.* Akron, OH: Principia.

Kantor, J.R. (1947). *Problems of physiological psychology.* Akron, OH: Principia.

Kantor, J.R. (1950). *Psychology and logic* (vol II). Akron, OH: Principia.

Kantor, J.R. (1953). *Logic of modern science*. Akron, OH: Principia.

Kantor, J.R. (1957). Events and constructs in the science of psychology: Philosophy—banished and recalled. *The Psychological Record, 7*, 55–60.

Kantor, J.R. (1958). *Interbehavioral psychology: A sample of scientific system construction*. Akron, OH: Principia.

Kantor, J.R. (1963–1969). *The scientific evolution of psychology and other sciences*. Akron, OH: Principia.

Kantor, J.R. (1969). Scientific psychology and specious philosophy. *The Psychological Record, 19*, 15–27.

Kantor, J.R. (1970). An analysis of the experimental analysis of behavior (TEAB). *Journal of the Experimental Analysis of Behavior, 13*, 101–108.

Kantor, J.R. (1977). *Psychological linguistics*. Akron, OH: Principia.

Kantor, J.R. (1981). *Interbehavioral philosophy.* Akron, OH: Principia.

Kantor, J.R. (1982). *Cultural psychology.* Akron, OH: Principia.

Kantor, J.R. (1983). *Tragedy and the event continuum.* Akron, OH: Principia.

Kantor, J.R., & Smith, N.W. (1975). *The science of psychology: An interbehavioral survey.* Akron, OH: Principia.

Kazdin, A.E. (2011). *Single-case research designs: Methods for clinical and applied settings* (2nd ed.). Oxford: Oxford University Press.

Kim, J., Sprangler, T.L., & Gutter, M.S. (2016). Extended families: Support, socialization, and stress. *Family and Consumer Research Journal, 45,* 104–118.

Kirkpatrick, M., Akers, J., & Rivera, G. (2019). Use of behavioral skills training with teachers: A systematic review. *Journal of Behavioral Education, 28,* 344–361.

Laraway, S., Snycerski, S., Michael, J., & Poling, A. (2003). Motivating operations and terms to describe them: Some further refinements. *Journal of Applied Behavior Analysis, 36*(3), 407–414.

Marr, J. (1996). Method and theory in memory; or, how many rooms are there in the Mad Hatter's house? *The Behavior Analyst, 19,* 89–90.

McHugh, L., Barnes-Holmes, Y., & Barnes-Holmes, D. (2004). Perspective-taking as relational responding: A developmental profile. *The Psychological Record, 54,* 115–144.

Michael, J. (1993). Establishing operations. *The Behavior Analyst, 16,* 191–206.

Montoya-Rodríguez, M.M., Molina, F.J., & McHugh, L. (2017). A review of relational frame theory research into deictic relational responding. *The Psychological Record,* 67, 569–579.

Mostafa, T., Gambaro, L., & Joshi, H. (2018). The impact of complex family structure on child well-being: Evidence from siblings. *Journal of Marriage and Family, 80,* 902–918.

Novak, G. (2012). Precursors to perspective taking. In L. McHugh & I. Stewart (Eds.), *The self and perspective-taking: Contributions and applications from modern behavioral science* (pp.89–105). Oakland, CA: Context Press.

Observer (1969). Comments and queries: The basis fallacy in psychology. *The Psychological Record, 19*, 645–648.

Palmer, D.C. (1991). A behavioral interpretation of memory. In L.J. Hayes & P.N. Chase (Eds.), *Dialogues on verbal behavior: The first international institute on verbal relations* (pp.261–279). Oakland, CA: Context Press.

Parrott, L.J. (1983a). On the differences between Skinner's radical behaviorism and Kantor's interbehaviorism. *Mexican Journal of Behavior Analysis, 9*, 95–115.

Parrott, L.J. (1983b). Perspectives on knowing and knowledge. *The Psychological Record, 33(2)*, 171–184.

Parrott, L.J. (1983c). Systematic foundations for the concept of private events: A critique. In N.W. Smith, P.T. Mountjoy, & D.H. Ruben (Eds.), *Reassessment in psychology: The interbehavioral alternative* (pp.251–268). Lanham, MD: University Press of America.

Parrott, L.J. (1984). Listening and understanding. *The Behavior Analyst, 7*, 29–39.

Parrott, L.J. (1986a). On the role of postulation in the analysis of inapparent events. In H.W. Reese & L.J. Parrott (Eds.), *Behavior science: Philosophical, methodological, and empirical advances* (pp.35–60). Mahwah, NJ: L. Erlbaum Associates.

Parrott, L.J. (1986b). Substitution and reference. In P.N. Chase & L.J. Parrott (Eds.), *Psychological aspects of language*. Springfield, IL: Charles Thomas.

Peterson, S., & Neef, N. (2019). Functional behavior assessment. In J.O. Cooper, T.E. Heron, & W.L. Heward (Eds.), *Applied behavior analysis* (3rd ed., pp.627–654). Boston: Pearson.

Piaget, J., & Inhelder, B. (1972). *The psychology of the child.* New York: Basic Books.

Plumb, J.C., Stewart, I., Dahl, J., & Lundgren, T. (2009). In search of meaning: Values in modern clinical behavior analysis. *The Behavior Analyst, 32*, 85–103.

Pronko, N.H. (1980). *Psychology from the standpoint of an interbehaviorist.* Pacific Grove, CA: Brooks/Cole.

Ribes, E. (2020). Human behavior is referential behavior. In M. Fryling, R.A. Rehfeldt, J. Tarbox, & L.J. Hayes (Eds.), *Applied behavior analysis of language and cognition: Concepts and principles for practitioners* (pp.94–114). Oakland, CA: New Harbinger.

Robles, T.F. (2014). Marital quality and health: Implications for marriage in the 21st century. *Current Directions in Psychological Science, 23,* 427–432.

Rosales-Ruiz, J., & Baer, D.M. (1997). Behavioral cusps: A developmental and pragmatic concept for behavior analysis. *Journal of Applied Behavior Analysis, 30,* 533–544.

Sandoz, E. (2020). Interbehavior as a clinical focus in CBS: A response to Hayes and Fryling (2019). *Journal of Contextual Behavioral Science, 18,* 273–275.

Santos-Nunes, M., Narciso, I., Vieira-Santos, S., & Roberto, M.S. (2018). Adoptive versus mixed families: Child adjustment, parenting stress and family environment. *Journal of Child and Family Studies*, 27, 1858–1869.

Skinner, B.F. (1938). *The behavior of organisms: An experimental analysis*. New York: Appleton-Century-Crofts.

Skinner, B.F. (1945). An operational analysis of psychological terms. Reprinted in *Cumulative Record* (1961), pp.272–286. New York: Appleton-Century-Crofts.

Skinner, B.F. (1953). *Science and human behavior.* New York: Free Press.

Skinner, B.F. (1957). *Verbal behavior.* New York: Appleton-Century-Crofts.

Skinner, B.F. (1969). *Contingencies of reinforcement: A theoretical analysis.* New York: Appleton-Century-Crofts.

Skinner, B.F. (1971). *Beyond freedom and dignity.* New York: Knopf.

Skinner, B.F. (1974). *About behaviorism.* New York: Knopf.

Skinner, B.F. (1978). Why I am not a cognitive psychologist. In B.F. Skinner (Ed.), *Reflections of behaviorism and society* (pp.97–112). Hoboken, NJ: Prentice Hall.

Skinner, B.F. (1983). Intellectual self-management in old age. *The American Psychologist, 38,* 239–244.

Skinner, B.F., & Vaughn, M.E. (1983). *Enjoy old age: A practical guide.* New York: Norton & Company.

Verplanck, W.S. (1970). Comments and queries: An "overstatement" on psychological research: What is a dissertation? *The Psychological Record, 20,* 119–122.

Vilardaga, R., Estévez, A., Levin, M.E., & Hayes, S.C. (2012). Deictic relational responding, empathy, and experiential avoidance as predictors of social anhedonia: Further contributions from relational frame theory. *The Psychological Record, 62,* 409–432.

Wolkenstein, L., Schönenberg, M., Schirm, E., & Hautzinger, M. (2011). I can see what you feel, but I can't deal with it: Impaired theory of mind in depression. *Journal of Affective Disorders, 132,* 104–111.

Wyman Battalon, A., Farr, R.H., Brodzinsky, D.M., & McRoy, R.G. (2019). Socializing children about family structure: Perspectives of lesbian and gay adoptive parents. *Journal of GLBT Family Studies, 15,* 235–255.

Zuckerman, P. (2015). *Living the secular life: New answers to old questions.* New York: Penguin Books.

Linda J. Hayes, PhD, is a Distinguished International Professor at the University of Nevada, Reno. She cofounded the behavior analysis program at the University of Nevada, Reno; and has served two terms as president of the Association for Behavior Analysis International. She has published works on behavior theory and philosophy from an interbehavioral perspective for four decades.

Mitch J. Fryling, PhD, is professor and associate dean in the college of education at California State University, Los Angeles. He has authored and coauthored many scholarly publications, primarily in the area of behavioral theory and philosophy, especially as it pertains to complex human behavior and system development in behavior analysis. He is current editor of *The Psychological Record.*

MORE BOOKS from NEW HARBINGER PUBLICATIONS

UNDERSTANDING AND APPLYING RELATIONAL FRAME THEORY

Mastering the Foundations of Complex Language in Our Work and Lives as Behavior Analysts

APPLIED BEHAVIOR ANALYSIS RESEARCH MADE EASY

A Handbook for Practitioners Conducting Research Post-Certification

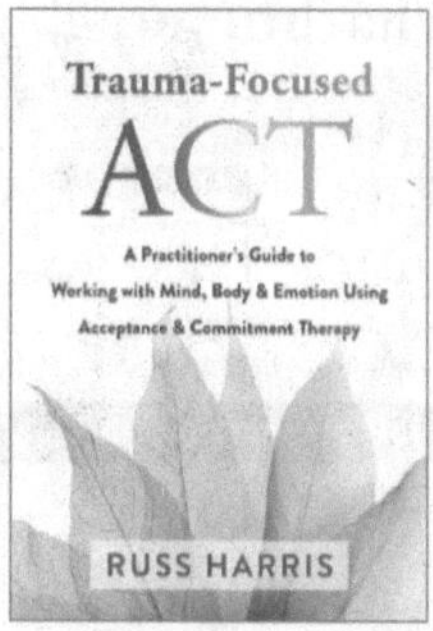

TRAUMA-FOCUSED ACT

A Practitioner's Guide to Working with Mind, Body, and Emotion Using Acceptance and Commitment Therapy

A CLINICIAN'S GUIDE TO TEACHING MINDFULNESS

The Comprehensive Session-by-Session Program for Mental Health Professionals and Health Care Providers

Back Cover Material

A comprehensive guide to understanding and applying interbehaviorism

By providing a naturalistic foundation to scientific methods and research, Jacob Robert Kantor's theory of *interbehaviorism* marked an essential and groundbreaking contribution to the behavioral sciences. This volume offers a complete outline of Kantor's pioneering theory, and uncovers the profound effects it has in applied domains such as perspective taking, feelings and emotions, interpersonal relationships, and more.

In this comprehensive book, you'll find an overview of the science and philosophy of interbehaviorism, as well as up-to-date research and modern applications. You'll also discover how Kantor's theory relates to human development, linguistic behavior, memory, values, and ethics. Whether you're a behavior analyst, contextual behavior scientist, student of behavior analysis, or simply interested in the history of the behavioral sciences, this book is an important addition to your professional library.

"A valuable contribution to the understanding of J.R. Kantor's philosophy.... This book should be required reading for students of behavior analysis."—Maria E.

Malott, PhD, CEO of the Association for Behavior Analysis International

Linda J. Hayes, PhD, is a Distinguished International Professor at the University of Nevada, Reno. She cofounded the behavior analysis program at the University of Nevada, Reno; and has served two terms as president of the Association for Behavior Analysis International.

Mitch J. Fryling, PhD, is professor and associate dean in the college of education at California State University, Los Angeles. He has authored many scholarly publications, primarily in the area of behavioral theory and philosophy. He is current editor of *The Psychological Record.*

A

C

D

E

F

K

Q

R

S

www.ingramcontent.com/pod-product-compliance
Lightning Source LLC
LaVergne TN
LVHW031614210926
848480LV00011B/1482
* 9 7 8 1 0 3 8 7 7 9 1 5 1 *